Illustrated with antique advertisements for nerve ointment,
performing cats, Bayer heroin, a clairvoyant physician,
an exploding cigar, and a beer dispenser
for the dashboard of your car.

Brisk Verse

Healthful. Invigorating. Good for reading aloud to friends and associates, neighbors, colleagues, bartenders, passersby, even strangers in libraries or on airplanes. One copy of this book will make you the life of the party, a welcome guest in any home, a person of fine taste who also relishes a good time.

GARRISON KEILLOR

Prairie Home Productions • Minneapolis, MN

First Edition

Library of Congress Control Number: 2024907287

ISBN 979-8-9882818-3-2

Cover and art design by David Provolo

Credits

p. 38 "Smedley's Chillie Paste" comes from the Ephemera Collection. QV: Advertising: 1850–1920 and is licensed under the Creative Commons Attribution 4.0 International license.

p. 134 "Climax Plug 1894 Advertisement" by Infrogmation of New Orleans (Flickr) is licensed under CC BY 2.0.

All other illustrations are in the public domain.

CONTENTS

Float Your Boat

My Baby

Supper

Murals

Corinne

Breakfast

My Violist and Me

May

Spring

Daughter

Summer Night

Stick with Me

Minnesota

Geology

Kansas

Amazon

Poem for Jenny

L.A.

Minneapolis

St. Paul Blues

Hymn to the Farm

The Bells of Minnesota

O Columbia, the gem of the ocean,
The home of the brave and the free
The home of Jergens Hand Lotion
And Lipton's Heart-Healthy tea.
With her garlands of victory around her,
When so proudly she bore her gallant crew,
A Home Depot granite kitchen counter
Will resist rust stains and scratches too.

The Star-Spangled Banner bring forward
O'er Columbia's true sons let it wave
When there's clothing to be ordered.
Shop at Walmart and you'll save.
May thy service united ne'er sever
But hold to their colors so true
Amazon will triumph forever
And Best Buy is there to wait on you.

FOREWORD

I blew away most of my youth writing bad poetry—long lugubrious lamentations about unbelonging in a crass uncaring commercial world of cutthroat competition that offended my delicate sensibilities—but when I hit 27 I became a grown-up, was married, had a kid, a car, a house with an address where bills were left on the Welcome mat, and I was forced to find my vocation in radio, working an early morning shift, where I learned that lugubriosity was of no earthly use to me. The audience was sleepy and not in need of narcissism. They were farmers, clerks, teachers, truckers, had work to do, and they needed something brisk to awaken them and arouse them to the prospects of the day. They needed cheering up.

My theme song was the Mills Brothers' "Bugle Call Rag" and I spun Tex-Mex and klezmer, polkas and patriotic songs, doo-wop and bebop, jug bands and gospel quartets, tossing in a tap dancer here, a jaw harpist there, Bach, "Help Me, Rhonda," Caruso, calypso, bel canto, singing belugas, blues guitarists, the Boswell Sisters, and now and then a poem. It started, I believe, when a man named Fred Petters from St. Cloud asked me to wish his wife a happy anniversary and I recited Shakespeare's "Let me not to the marriage of true minds admit impediments" and I got a thank-you note from Rosemary, the wife, that suggested that children were sort of impediments but they were doing very well, thank you. So I started writing poems again, but not ones about alienation, bereavement, chaos, despair, existential fatalism, grinding hopelessness, impotence, etcetera, but jazzy ones like "My eyes get misty when I think of Julie Christie; if a man wished to be kissed he would want it to be her lips." I had an audience, why not talk to them? I wrote rhymed metrical verse so it would grab their attention and I ventured outside standard poetic topics, love, beauty, natural wonder, blah blah blah, to outlying areas, sex, flatulence, urination, good manners, suicide, linguini, bikinis, bratwurst. I employed poetry to entertain the rank and file rather than try to impress fellow poets. It made me feel good about myself, a Sanctified Brethren boy slipping the bonds of sanctity to make people feel good.

I did radio for years and then suddenly, for no good reason, I was very old. I find that life quickens when there's less in the tank, so you step lively, get to the point, wake up and die right. You're too old to hold grudges or get in a fury about politics or imagine that maple syrup causes multiple sclerosis or that stepping on a crack can break your mother's back. Past 65 it's the age of gratitude, so seek out the beautiful, virtuous, loving, humorous, and true, and let the younger people obsess over the meaningless and the acquisition of nonsense and trash.

In 1994 I started up *The Writer's Almanac,* which included a poem—Mary Oliver, Maxine Kumin, Theodore Roethke, Billy Collins, W.S. Merwin, Grace Paley, Louis Jenkins, etc., etc.—which I chose for its clarity—poems that could be grasped and enjoyed by a person whipping up an omelet with small children tugging at your pant legs— and because many stations broadcast *TWA* at 7 or 8 a.m., I excluded poems of dread, cynicism, agony, meditations on evil, poems about death, especially the death of small children. Too early in the morning for that. And over the years, as listeners wrote to tell me they looked forward to the daily poem, I felt I was performing a public service. Shakespeare's Sonnet 29, for example, which details his miseries and regrets and then *For thy sweet love remember'd such wealth brings that then I scorn to change my state with kings,* a useful reminder in the morning while facing a difficult day: the redemptive power of love.

Back in college we never used the word "useful" when discussing *The Waste Land* or Berryman's *Dream Songs*—we considered great art to live beyond such a mundane standard—and I pondered plenty of poetry that, I realized later, was written by poets who were falling-down drunk or batshit crazy and looking for the rat poison, and I'm sorry but you don't go to the locked ward of the loony bin to figure out how to live your life.

In my twenties I stumbled along writing unreadable stuff and thinking of life as meaningless, which in my case was true at the time, and then I stumbled into radio and started enjoying *talking* to people, and, as it turned out, depression passed me by entirely, and now I could no more write about desperation than I could write about being an Alabama sharecropper locked in the Mobile jail for drunkenness and possession of a deadly weapon. I've never been to Mobile. I quit drinking long ago. My only deadly weapon was sarcasm.

I like the poem that you write as a gift to someone, such as:

This is a limerick for Jenny
Whose virtues are golden and many,
Whose faults are few,
Perhaps one or two,
Though right now I can't think of any.

And if you're ambitious, a poem, the first letters of whose lines spell out the recipient's name:

Elegant, energetic, entertaining, and effusive,
Rarely repetitive and hardly ever tedious,
In every situation, she makes full use of
Comedy and command of all medias,
Always cool, she keeps turning the page,
Roving restlessly on the nightclub stage.
Happily at work while highly wary
Of jerks and opportunists, always very
Diligent in serving the sad and solitary,

Entertaining therapists with her private episodes,
Sail on, sweet soloist, Erica Rhodes.

I wrote poems for many of my doctors, including my cousin Dan who likely saved my life when he heard wheeziness listening to me tell the news from Lake Wobegon on the radio and shipped me to Mayo to get cut open and have my mitral valve sewn up. When someone saves your life, you don't write a meditation on death. I wrote:

A diligent doctor named Dan
Is stuck with being the man
To urge compliance
With medical science
Which you won't though you should and you can.

And recently, for Dr. John Chen:

My eye doctor, good Dr. Chen
Did magic recently when
He lasered one eye
Briefly, now I
Who couldn't read signs
Or books or the *Times*
Can read them clearly again.
And this, for me,
Who am literary
Makes Chen worth a poem with a pen.

I wrote my mournful poems when I was young and in good health but as I got into my sixties and had scary experiences such as seizures that sent me to a neurologist, I was forced to become an optimist.

There is a neurologist, Jim,
Whose diagnoses are grim—
So he opens each visit
By asking, "How is it?"
And singing an uplifting hymn.
He gave me a pill for a start
That let me understand art.
One pill from the bottle,
Now I read Aristotle
And I think I am René Descartes.

In other words, Folks With Strokes Can Still Tell Jokes.

I departed from the poetry we studied in college, Auden, Berryman, Crane, Dickey, Eliot, et al., and toward rhymed metrical verse because rhyme is an aid to memory and I like to have poems in my head, and also meter creates an illusion of order within which loony gestures and inspirational asides have more impact.

I quit going to poetry readings long ago. Too much dramatic exhibition of keen sensitivity, too many obligatory sighs of wonderment. I much prefer laughter. Nobody fakes laughter. I give these to you in hopes that you might like some enough to read one aloud to a person sitting nearby. You just say, "Listen to this," and read the poem and if it lands right, you've created a pleasant moment, and then we go on to something else.

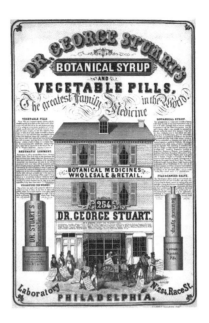

---

1. SAGE

WALKERS

It's good to take a brisk walk every day,
And it will do wonders to improve your mood.
And you may run into Claude Monet,
Or Chopin humming his *Tristesse* étude.
Jack Benny, Bessie Smith, stand not far apart,
Bill and Marilyn Monroe, you never know,
The Duke of Earl, Amelia Earhart,
Vincent van Gogh looking at the snow,
Melville whose book you meant to read,
Out walking, despite all he's been through.
"To comprehend a nectar requires sorest need,"
Said Emily Dickinson. (She's here, too.)
Life is hard. Lord, the miseries we bear
And yet it's good to get out in the open air.

Manners

Columbus sailed the ocean blue
Back in 1492.
He sailed across and spotted land,
Saw people in the forest and
Called them Indians because
He had no idea where he was.
India was a wild guess.
When in doubt, declare success.
Leif Ericsson centuries before
Landed in Labrador
And saw natives behind the trees.
He didn't call them Lebanese.
We don't have Leif Ericsson Day
Or a university or statue.
He was a Viking. He knew that you
Come and go. Don't stay.
You resume seafaring.
He wasn't in search of gold
Or slaves who could be sold,
He only wanted herring.

STOICISM

They love you still, your mom and dad.
   You may not think so, but they w.
They gave you all the love they had
   Though they were human, that is true.

And they had trouble with their folks
   That they kept quiet from your ears.
Underneath the family jokes
   Was shouting, silence, many tears.

If childhood history makes you blue,
   Thinking of your parents' mess,
Let the misery end with you
   And treat your kids with tenderness.

Do not agitate your soul
Over things you can't control.
Assume the best of those you meet,
Forgive mistakes, ill will, deceit.
Practice kindness, open doors.
Forgive the idiots and jerks.
Mortify them with good works.
They're for God's reckoning, not yours.

CLEANLINESS

As we see mirth and beauty at a concert or a play,
There are people with whom we socialize
Who are sneezing and coughing and so along the way
It's important to stop and sanitize.
Your grandma told you, your mother told you too,
And your sweetheart is trying to tell you yet;
A thousand and one times it's been pounded into you:
Wash your hands, every chance you get.
When embracing your sweetheart, why pass on disease,
And in weeks to come as you hover
Over the deathbed and whisper, "Rest in peace,"
You know you are to blame who meant to love her.
Sonnets have been written about following your heart
But this one is wiser: use sanitizer.

ADVICE

I seldom offer advice
Unless it is requested
But this is expert advice,
Proven, well-tested,
Based on firsthand knowledge,
Not something I picked up in college.

Say "please" and "thank you,"
Mind your p's and q's.
Don't waste money on bad food
But never buy cheap shoes.
A stitch in time saves nine;
Pride goeth before a fall.
On the other hand, don't put yourself down.
Don't slouch, walk tall.
It's usually simpler to tell the truth;
Time brings all things to light.
On the other hand, people love stories
If it's fiction, make it fit tight.
This too shall pass;
Life is not fair.
Don't chew with your mouth open
And always wear clean underwear.
And no matter how life goes,
One thing is true and you know it:
Don't pick your nose.
Pull out a hanky and blow it.

There are exceptions to every rule
Except this one: a fool
And his money are easily parted.
Want to hear about fools?
Don't get me started.

Be kind to strangers.
Remember: whatever you do
For children you do for the Lord
Who will shine His light on you.
Speak softly, they'll listen.
Insults? Let them pass.
Anger will likely come back
And bite you in the ass.
Wake up in the morning
With a cheerful heart.
Pretend not to notice
If a loved one lets a fart.
The sun also rises
And the stars disappear
So be thankful for today
And all we have down here.
Avoid impulsive decisions.
Discuss it with someone first
And make a few revisions
So the bubble doesn't burst.

And don't pick your nose
Unless you're alone with the window closed
And the shades pulled so nobody can look through it.
Don't do it.

So many young men were succeeding,
Were admired and even revered—
When suddenly at a very important meeting
Their index finger disappeared.

Suddenly you'll be caught
And even when you stop,
Suddenly your stock will drop.
Is this a good idea? No, it's snot.
People will dismiss you and they won't miss you.
Use a tissue.

EULOGY

Somebody said that it couldn't be done, but he with a smile replied

That maybe it couldn't but he would be one who wouldn't say so till he tried.

So he buckled right in with a bit of a grin

And his screwdriver touched a live wire,

And he let out a cry and proceeded to die

In a shower of sparks and fire.

And the people who gave the eulogy

Spoke of honor and love and ambition.

They spoke well of the dead, and nobody said,

"Why didn't he call an electrician?"

What Goes Around

It was back in nineteen eighty-five
The boys and I came up here
With our rifles and tent to Bemidji we went
To hunt the whitetail deer.

We drove into the woods and pitched our tent
The night was crisp and clear.
We built us a fire and as the flames leaped higher
We drank up half the beer.

We grilled the steaks and reminisced
About what great hunters we had been
And we dealt out the cards and played a game of Hearts,
And then we all turned in.

I awoke about 2 a.m.
Because I needed to pee.
And just my luck, there stood a buck,
Looking straight at me.

I heard a rustling in the brush
And there stood a dozen whitetails.
And all at once I saw they had our guns
And they were drunk on Moosehead ale.

What can you do about drunken deer
Who are armed and dangerous?
And I started to pray that the deer would go away
And not start hunting us.

And I started in to preach from the Gospel of John
That God is love and He exists.
And there beneath the trees the deer dropped to their knees
And they became Methodists.

And then I heard the old buck pray:
"I thank you, Lord, that I believe.
Such gratitude I feel and I thank you for the meal
We are about to receive."

He aimed his rifle straight at me
As soon as he said, "Amen."
I let out a scream and awoke from the dream
And I never went hunting again.

That was thirty years ago north of Bemidji
And I tell you honestly
Whenever I eat a piece of red meat
That deer is aiming at me.

4 A.M.

The need of solitude
Is basic, like food.
Teachers, preachers,
All of God's creatures,
Mothers as well,
And health personnel,
Farmers, writers,
Former prizefighters,
Require periods of silence
When a phone call is a form of violence
And a knock on the door is sheer mayhem.
So I arise around 4 a.m.
And I find it very pleasant
That nobody else is present:
Coffee, paper, and a pencil,
All that are essential.
I hear the chirping of the birds
And in my head, a flock of words,
So many lovely ways to say:
Thank you for another day.

Midnight Train

I hear the whistle of the midnight train
Heading 'cross the prairie through the driving rain
With a boxcar full of hoboes dying of TB
And a chain gang and a dozen refugees.

Up front in the club car, listening to the whistle blow,
Buddy Holly, Janis Joplin, Marilyn Monroe,
Virginia Woolf, and Elvis, his face is ghastly white,
Singing "Are You Lonesome Tonight?"

The club car's cold and dark, the gin's been put away.
Franz Kafka sits with JFK and a dozen men in gray
Who gave their lives for the Lost Cause and Robert E. Lee
And women from the Triangle Shirtwaist factory.

And the train raced on, and the lonesome whistle blew
For F. Scott and the Edmund Fitzgerald crew
And the tribes who were wiped out on the western frontier,
And then I saw there was no engineer.

It's the everlasting passage of human suffering,
No one is secure from the grief that it can bring.
I watch it go by until the red lights disappear,
Then I come home, put my arms around you, dear.

"What were you doing out there?" you say.
"Looking at the stars," I reply and turn away.
Supper's on the table. Life goes on.

The midnight train is past and gone.
Someday it may stop for me, I suppose,
But I raise my cup, which overflows,
Here's to family and friends good and true,
Here's to the children. Here's to you.

Homemade bread! Oh, boy!

Give your children real homemade bread; see what
an appetite it will give them. Be sure of good
bread. Make it with Yeast Foam or Magic Yeast.

Magic Yeast   Yeast Foam
Just the same
except in name

Send for booklet,
"The Art of Baking Bread"

NORTHWESTERN YEAST CO.
CHICAGO

Hard Thoughts

Not all hard thoughts need be expressed—
The early death you've always feared,
Your heart pounding in your chest,
The feeling that your hair looks weird,
You're getting fat, the plane might fall
Screaming out of the sky and plow
Into the mountain and we all
Die—let's not discuss it now.
Let's talk about last night instead,
The old hotel beside the park,
Mahler's Fourth that we heard in bed,
What happened later in the dark.
    Not all hard thoughts need be expressed.
    Know that I love you. Forget the rest.

You Are Not Alone

When love is lost there's not much to say
Except life will never again be miraculous.
I see the young woman in this café,
Alone, her eyes luminous
With tears, I wish for a way
To tell her: *You're not alone.*
You're not alone.
What you feel now we too have known,
Hundreds of us.

The one you lost is gone so here you are
Living in a sad movie but it has an end
When you will see: the sky is very forgiving,
The moon rising wants to be your friend.
You will be embraced by summer rains,
The chittering of birds in the trees,
The luxury of tall grasses remains,
And the persistence of our species.
Listen to them as they pass,
People chattering on the phone,
Little kids released from class,
The lovers walking hand in hand,
The ballet lady posing on the grass,
The long line at the ice cream stand,
We are yours, we are your own,
Find your place in the marching band.
You are not alone.
Don't be alone.

Advice to Graduates

Be happy. Be bold. That's what my advice is:
And if it's happiness for which you hunger,
Don't wait until midlife to have your crisis.
Get it out of the way when you're younger.
Don't wait until you're older and at the pinnacle
And people stand at the dais and hail your
Achievements. I hate to sound cynical,
But youth is the best time for a magnificent failure.
You won't learn this from reading Plato or Socrates
But rather than Clueless, why not go for Really Bad?
Better to be a fool than one of the mediocrities.
And it'll bring you closer to your dad.
    Waste your inheritance. Fate must be fulfilled.
    He's waiting to forgive you. That fatted calf needs to be killed.

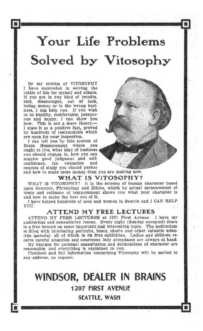

BREVITY

I've been around in the show biz
Played every theater there is,
And carnivals and bazaars and the occasional church.
I've guessed weights, been a freak,
Was glad to sing or dance or speak
And then sit outside at a table and sell the merch.

I used to dance with Merce Cunningham
On Kate Smith's radio program,
She sang "God Bless America" as we waved Old Glory.
I used to travel with Pavarotti
Back when he had a muscleman body
And wore leopard-skin briefs in *Il Trovatore*.

I told fortunes, was an acrobat,
I danced while the fat lady passed the hat,
I handed out free saltines and sold lemonades.
Sold souvenirs and hats and visors,
Flyswatters and vegetable dicers
And tell me which one of these cards is the queen of spades.

I've played the Garden, not the Madison,
The Garden Lounge of the St. Paul Radisson,
And I've played some Bowls, the kind where they use pins.
I did shows that were a riot
And some that were extremely quiet
To salesmen on Monday nights in Holiday Inns.

I have crashed and I have burned,
But there're some things I have learned
In my long and checkered performing history.
A couple precepts you should know
If you wish to do a show
And I'm going to pass them on absolutely free.

Whenever you talk, whenever you sing:
Don't be too much of a good thing.
Wisdom is wiser in smaller pieces.
Don't make a sermon into a thesis.
Brevity is the soul of wit.
Go out there, get ahead, then quit.
If people clap and shout Encore,
Just remember: less is more.

Less is more, what more can I say?
A hero is a man who went away.
Today your praises would be sung
If only you'd died when you were young.
Jim Morrison, Elvis, Otis,
Jimi Hendrix: they all showed us
The best career move is to go away.

Sing your songs, tell your jokes,
And holler, "Thank you. Good night, folks."
Don't come back for a closing hymn. O
Head for the door and jump in the limo.
Leave them wanting more, okay?
Don't hang around for the Q & A,
The autographs, the adulation,

The fascination of ego inflation.

Pack your bag, grab the cash,

Put on dark glasses and fake moustache,

Out the door, jump in the car,

And go back to being who you are.

Every star and every hero

Eventually becomes a big fat zero.

So don't come back for a final bow.

Leave the building. Go. Now.

The standing O you were hoping for

Is your audience heading for the door.

Anyway, that's enough from me.

I'm history.

LITTLE DOROTHY'S ADVICE

He came home from work in a fury
His boss made him suicidal,
And Mother yelled at him, "Hurry,
We're late for Jim's trombone recital
And then the church fund drive."
And up to the rooftop poor Father fled
Intending to take a swan dive
When little Dorothy stepped up and said:

"Don't jump off the roof, Dad.
You'll just make a mess in the yard.
The petunias are almost in blossom
And Mother's been working so hard.
And we'll have to go into grief therapy
And share feelings for six weeks or more.
Why not try carbon monoxide?
It's worked for others before."

So Daddy came down from the rooftop
But Mom had the keys to the car.
He couldn't take poison, the thought made him sick,
And a BB gun just won't do the trick.
The sleeping pills in the bottle
Weren't as strong as he'd need.
He grabbed some rope and headed downstairs
When Dorothy stepped up to plead:

"Don't hang yourself in the basement.
The water pipes can't take the weight.
There won't be hot water for showers
And tonight I have a big date.
Why hang yourself in the basement?
It's so much better with gas.
Just stick your head in the oven, Dad.
It's always worked in the past."

So Daddy came up from the basement
And he opened the oven door,
But Maddy was baking a pie, what a shame.
You can't bake a pie if you blow out the flame.
The knives were all dull in the pantry,
The arsenic in low supply.
So he took an electric fan to the bathroom
When Dorothy started to cry:

"Don't drop a fan in the bathtub, Dad.
It'll probably knock out the power.
And 'Who Wants to Be a Millionaire?'
Comes on in half an hour.
We'd die if we had to miss it
So please won't you give us a break?
Just take a walk to the park, Dad.
And there you can jump in the lake."

So Daddy went walking down to the park
Planning to jump in the lake
But before he reached the last act of his drama
He recalled the words of the great Dalai Lama

Who said, "It's darkest before the dawn,"
So he decided he ought to go on
Living and not drop dead
And was grateful to Dorothy who had said:

"Don't jump off of the roof, Dad."
She had saved his life, the sweet child.
And the trombone recital wasn't so bad
And he and Mom reconciled.
And the next day at work when he went back,
The boss was gone. A heart attack.
So there were no more miserable days,
And his widow gave Dad a generous raise,
Which just goes to show: Avoid agony,
Things will get better, just wait and see.
The sun will shine, we'll be in the clover,
So do not die until your life's over.

EIGHTY

I never wanted to be known for longevity.
Au contraire. I aimed for brevity.
A short brilliant tragically interrupted career
But instead it has gone on for eighty years.

I wanted to be brief, dear heart,
Like Buddy Holly or Amelia Earhart,
A shooting star, a beautiful flash,
But my plane did not crash.

I kept on and on keeping on,
Planting a garden, mowing the lawn,
Now I see that the heroes are gone
And I'm eating breakfast on another dawn.

I might've been immortal but I failed to decease.
I do love this sausage, think I'll have another piece.

In the Reference Room

To dance in a meadow under the moon
Is a joy and a pleasure, surely.
But there's no place like the reference room
When I am feeling poorly.
To sit at a table surrounded by nerds
At work on their master's degrees
While I write a limerick that starts with the words,
"A man can stand up when he pees."
They're in economics, they're categorizing
Ideas with extrinsic fluency,
Analyzing and strategizing,
While I am practicing truancy.
Men and women with Ph.D.s
Studying cheek to jowl
Like hundreds of mockingbirds parked in the trees
Surrounding me, the lone owl.
Learning only leads to more sorrow
While nonsense can bring us good cheer.
Why should we agonize over tomorrow?
Piss on it. Let's have a beer.

THE SECRET OF GENIUS

Every day Tolstoy sat down and penned
Page after page and did not cease
Until he had written "The End"
At the end of *War and Peace.*
Mrs. Melville sat at the table
And stirred the soup until it was thick
As Herman worked his little fable
Slowly into *Moby-Dick.*
Jane Austen had the ability
Even though she felt wretched as
She wrote *Sense and Sensibility*
To go on to *Pride and Prejudice.*
Dostoevsky over time
Found a punishment to fit the crime
And slowly as a centipede trots off
He wrote *The Brothers Karamazov.*
Mrs. Joyce cried out for bliss, "He's
Finally done it. He wrote *Ulysses.*"
James had supper, took a break,
And started in on *Finnegans Wake.*
Slowly, slowly, page by page
Emerge the epics of the age;
You write and take your time: you're liable
To make a good book, if not a Bible.
Churchill with his memoirs written
Started in on a history of Britain
Covering more than a millennium,
Starting every day around ten a.m.
So do your writing, day after day,
Page after page, forge ahead,
And after you have passed away
You'll be famous, if not read.

MOVE OVER

Same old story for me and you:
It's out with the old and in with the new.
You can sing your song, and do your dance
But there're people in the wings with a hook in their hands.
Move over, old dog, the new dog's moving in.

You're rising fast, a big sensation,
Your face on the cover of a major publication,
Two years later you're on tour on a bus
Playing bass and feeling anonymous,
Superannuated and annoyed,
No longer a star, just an asteroid.

You're king of the hill, chairman of the board,
Winner of the Mister Wonderful award,
Then you bang your head on the door, O Lord,
You're in assisted living in the Memory Ward.
Move over, old man, this is now and you are way back when.

Live your life and don't postpone
'Cause someday God's gonna call in the loan.
You may go to paradise or maybe not,
There may be smoke and the floor is hot.
Move over, sinner, and approach the Judgment Throne.

An Ode to Editors

I am an editor, and I do it well;
I make small revisions that ring the bell.
I edited Churchill's speeches for years;
He wrote "Blood and perspiration," I said, "Blood, sweat, and tears."

Francis Fitzgerald was mine; I liked him a lot.
I dropped the Francis and made him F. Scott.
Ernest Hemingway was broke, unknown, unemployed.
I gave him his name; he'd been Ernie Hemorrhoid.

I know what a difference small changes can make.
Gertrude Stein was Gladys, for goodness' sake.
Nobody gives us editors much credit.
Who was Bob Zimmerman before I made the edit?
A young guy from Hibbing who showed some promise.
I made him Dylan after Dylan Thomas.
He wrote "Mister Trombone," I made it "Tambourine."
I wrote "Highway 61 Revisited," it had been "Highway 14."

John Steinbeck taught math, wrote a book about shapes.
I changed it to *Wrath* and added the *Grapes*.
I edited a novel by Sinclair Lewis
About a small French town, I changed it to the U.S.

Allen Ginsberg came to me back in 1959.
He was writing a poem and had the first line:
"I saw the best minds of my generation, starving, hysterical,
   in their underwear."
I said, "Make it 'naked,' 'underwear' sounds square."

Jerry Garcia came to me, said, "I want to start a band.
Got a concert Saturday night out at Winterland."
He played me a demo tape, I listened, and I said,
"That's the worst band I ever heard. I'll be grateful when it's dead."

Tiny edits can make a fast into a feast.
Norman Mailer came to me with *The Naked and the Deceased*.
Did I get a footnote of acknowledgment?
If he wrote a thank-you note, it was never sent.

And Donald Trump: his first caps were blue,
And instead of MAGA, they said MAGOO.
His name was Tramp, but I put in the U.
Did he thank me? No, but I knew what to do,
I went to Dominion and put a small slide in
The voting machines I could adjust to widen
The margin of victory and I elected Joe Biden.

2. GREEN PARADISE

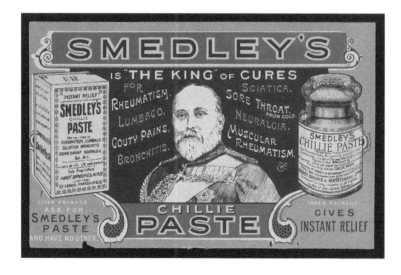

SPRING

O gentle spring that banished winter, our ill-tempered dad,
Who was never so nice to us as you are, dear spring, who sent
Us last Tuesday and Wednesday, the sweetest days we ever had,
And winter only yelled at us and who knew what he meant?

O spring, our mother, your greenness like a beautiful breast
And the lilacs and sunshine and no mosquitoes yet, and no green flies,
Your loveliness is almost more than someone from the Midwest
Can accept, but for the moment, we are in a sort of paradise.

Thank you for sending Dad away and all his lectures about duty
And character and preparedness—what a relief to lie
In your hammock, Mama, and get drunk on your beauty
And look at your kindly grasses and your benevolent sky.

Although Friday we got a thunderstorm with hailstones as big as a dime.
It was him, reminding us he is out there, biding his time.

Spring 2

Spring, sweet spring, the equinox,
It happens as a person walks
Outdoors and feels the juice
And life is easy again and loose
And the earth presents produce.
The playground is a riot of action
Now that the children can get traction.
Children skip and hop
Across the blacktop,
Singing at the sight of daylight
Like caged birds taking flight.
Sweaters and jackets slung
Over arms because spring has sprung.
People loiter and hang
Out because spring just sprang.
The sun is shining
And the patio is open for dining.

Green green green all around,
Crocuses coming out of the ground.
People smile and people sneeze
Expressing their innermost allergies.

All the world belongs to lovers,
They dance on grates and manhole covers
With simple syncopation
At the pleasure of God's creation.
Scat, doowop, hip-hop, bebop,
Love's rhythms never stop.

On the vernal equinox,

I comb my hair, pull up my socks,

Sitting with the other men,

Hoping she will sing again

And I will hear her when she sings.

Men do not decide these things.

I listen to the songs of birds

And I can hear her say the words,

"Roll up your pant cuffs, buckle your pants,

Take off your shoes and socks, let's dance."

SPRING 3

March and Lent and we march along on our spiritual journeys
As winter lingers and the world looks older and duller
And then the mailman brings the spring seed catalogue from Gurney's
And suddenly there is life and audacious color
And excitement rivaling Times Square or Las Vegas—
Blue Lake, Early Fortune, King of the Garden beans,
Stunning onions, phenomenal fennel, and big brutes of rutabagas,
And the beet that can't be beat: the extra-early Ruby Queens.
And O the tomatoes! The vegetable of pure joy!
From tasteless store-bought stuff, deliver us!
The Crimson Defender, and Pink Delight, and Big Boy,
And the Beef Eater—the tomato carnivorous.
     Lord, whose wisdom is all encompassing, whose word is ever valid,
     Give me one more summer, at least until July, when we'll have salad.

Summer Night

O summer, here you are sh-bop sh-bop yeah yeah whoa whoa
And we are driving around town tonight, hey hey hey
Windows open and the Beach Boys playing on the radio
And we'll have fun fun fun till Daddy takes the T-bird away,
Which Daddy will do and then we must Make Something of our lives
And climb the steep slope of success hauling ass like Sherpas
And become daddies ourselves and our good wives
Will frown if we drive anywhere without a clear purpose.
But tonight I am cruising for no reason around St. Paul
And it all comes back, those wild girls I used to hang
Around with when we had no place to go at all
Except around and around, the radio playing shang-a-lang
O baby baby, shoop shoop do you know what I mean
I'll be old again now but for a few minutes I was 18.

3. PERILS AND PITFALLS

Smoke Detectors

Insofar as you are able,
Whether you are man or boy, don't tamper with or disable
Or for that matter destroy
Smoke detectors in the lavatory,
It is in the category
Of a major faux pas
And prohibited by federal law.

Neither a garbage collector, gold prospector, Episcopal rector,
Cable TV director, police inspector, or Russian defector,
Either as a joke, or for love or glory,
Or because you need to smoke,
Should go to the lavatory
And be a smoke detector destroyer
Unless you have a very good lawyer.

It may do no harm
But the destruction will set off an alarm
That the detector has been destroyed
And passengers will be annoyed
And assume the culprit is armed
Or mentally unstable
And the plane'll make an emergency landing
And you'll be standing
Before a judge
And you won't like it much
To be sentenced to six months of license plate production
For smoke detector destruction.

CAPITALISM

You and I bought us a studio
Apartment, north side of Chicago,
But when we incorporate and issue stock
And thousands of investors flock
And the price goes from fifteen to fifty-five
We'll head on up the Lake Shore Drive.
We'll jack up the price by incurring debt
And get a house in Wilmette
And when the stock goes through the ceiling
We'll move to Deerfield, Northbrook, or Wheeling.

When the bubble expands like in the '80s
We'll move to Winnetka and buy a Mercedes
And finally wind up in Lake Forest
And then I suppose we'll get divorced.
You'll get the house, I'll get what remains:
A used Honda and a place in Des Plaines.
I'll date a waitress named LaVonne
And buy a bungalow in Oak Lawn.
When the company tanks, I pray to God
That the D.A. doesn't know much about fraud
And the jury acquits and I don't get
An 8x10 cell in Joliet.

Breakup Song

You thought my eyes were brown,

They're blue.

You forgot my birthday is April 5th.

The day passed with no gift.

On the 6th you apologized in shame

And gave me a card that misspelled my last name

And a pullover that was too small to pull

And you forgot I'm allergic to wool.

And that's why I gave you a shove

Into the dumpster of love.

And now your friends call me to say

You're homeless, sleeping in a doorway.

You've gone from a very lovely romance

To rummaging around in garbage cans

And panhandling on the corner.

Once you were current, now you're former.

Maybe someday you'll realize

The importance of knowing the color of your lover's eyes,

Her allergies, the day she was born,

And her last name is not Warren, it's Warn.

Now I see you've texted me three times this morning.

So I'm sending this warning:

I could get a restraining order from a court

So that if you so much as glance or snort

In my direction,

You go to an institution of correction.

In other words, we're done.

It was fun

But then you crossed
A line. Get lost.
Your eyes are green
And nevermore to be seen.
We're through.
Screw you
And your family too
And all you stand for.
I've locked the door.
Don't text or post.
You're toast.

ONLINE LOVE

I met you on the internet
In a chat room called Hard 2 Get.
Our two minds seemed to meld
We chatted and we LOLed
Though you're 18 and I'm 59
We were beautiful online.
All I know is your email address
And your screen name: Princess.
But it was awesome. OMG,
As a virtual world can be.
You sent me your JPG.
I checked you out on Instagram.
Wham bam, thank you, ma'am.
I didn't send you a photo of me.
Why should we rush into reality?
I said WFH but that ain't true,
My H is prison, AKA the zoo.
Ten years ago, don't know why,
I shot a man in Reno. But that's TMI.
Someday when I get off my butt
And exercise and lose this gut,
And I'm out of jail and back on the street
Then you and I will meet.
FYI, I dream about you at night,
Someday we'll have our own website.
Got another two years before parole,
Going to diet to save my soul.
I'll marry you ASAP.
We'll live in beautiful harmony.
Darling, you are my flame,
Got your picture in a frame,
My claim to fame,
I just wish I knew your name.

THE CREW

His name was Chesley B. Sullenberger the Third
Which for a pilot sounds absurd.
A pilot's name should be Buzz, Bill, or Chuck
But a name like Chesley may mean good luck.

He was flying an Airbus out of New York
When at 3,000 feet the engine lost torque.
His voice was calm as he sent out the word:
Chesley B. Sullenberger the Third—.

No time to maneuver or head for New Jersey;
The force of gravity shows no mercy,
And there was the river stretching for miles
So he said to his copilot, Jeffrey Skiles,
"We'll put it down here, don't look at the maps.
Bring the landing gear up and extend the flaps."
And the flight attendants prepared themselves:
Donna Dent, Sheila Dail, and Doreen Welsh.

Three hundred, two hundred, one hundred feet,
And he landed at the foot of 48th Street.
On the Hudson River he landed the bird,
Chesley B. Sullenberger the Third.

The plane did not sink, it lay on the river
And all aboard were safely delivered.
It could have been tragic but no deaths occurred
Thanks to Chesley B. Sullenberger the Third.

The next time you fly, glance in the cockpit
Where the captain and co-captain sit,
Ready to take you up and onward
Like Chesley B. Sullenberger the Third.

Take you off for a thousand miles
With officers like Jeffrey Skiles
And attendants who, in crisis, don't fail:
Donna Dent, Doreen Welsh, and Sheila Dail.

A Cautionary Tale

There was once a young man who left his home in Minnesota
And moved to L.A. to become important
For he had written a screenplay about growing up feeling unwanted
Which he could not show to members of his family.

So he hung out in West Hollywood with cool people
Who shaved their heads and wore major black eye shadow.
His screenplay was rejected but he became an influencer
With two million followers and a lucrative contract with Calvin Klein.

His screenplay had been about the emptiness of success
But now he could enjoy some excellent single-malt Scotch
And he owned a four-bedroom condo in Pacific Palisades
And was very cool right up to the night he was run over by a bus.

He was riding his e-scooter the wrong way in the left lane
Which can happen when you wear dark glasses and are rather absorbed
    in yourself
And now he lies in a care center not sure what happened or why.
So remember, young people, even if you're cool you should look both ways.

SPAGHETTI

There's no simple way to eat spaghetti.
I love to sing but employment isn't steady.
Every life has its share of perils.
You can't go through life singing Christmas carols.

You may have a B.A. or a Master's
But life is a series of minor disasters.
Your big career can crash in the ditch,
Anything can happen and you never know which.

There's no simple way to eat spaghetti.
You'll never have kids if you wait until you're ready.
Every life includes some regret.
There's always something that you manage to forget.

It's easier to eat ravioli
But you can't live on ravioli solely.
You also need some greens and beans
And you know what eating beans means.

Fettucine is hard and linguini.
And it's hard to tell Puccini from Rossini.
But macaroni and cheese can be eaten with ease
So give me an extra-large helping, please,
Before I've lost a
Taste for pasta.

THE BIG EXAM

Now I Lay Me
Down to Rest,
And Pray I'll Pass
Tomorrow's Test.

If I Have Failed to
Learn this Junk,
Then Probably
My Ship Has Sunk.

If I Should Cheat
And Copy Hers,
I Hope She Has
The Right Answers.

If I Should Pass
And Graduate
I Hope I Find
A Wealthy Mate

Whose Father Owns
A Chain of Malls
So I Won't Have
To Work At All.

If I Should Die
Before I Wake,
That's One Less Test
I'll Have to Take.
If I Should Die
And Go to Hell
I Hope My Teacher's
There as Well.

Boarding

Here is my photo ID.
See? It's me,
The same serious facial expression.
And it's a fact:
These bags have been in my possession
Since they were packed.
No one unknown has asked me to carry
Any foreign, dangerous, or incendiary
Object aboard this flight.
All right?

The metal detector shows no plastic explosive,
The sniffer dog detects no dose of
Reefer or cocaine.
The bank will confirm: I have good credit
And paid promptly what I owed.
My gas is unleaded
And my plumbing's up to code.
May I please board the plane?
I am flying to Maine
To visit family,
My brother Sam and his wife, Emily,
Who are, I can say without hesitance,
Legal residents,
Therapists with many clients,
In full compliance
With state and local regulations
And up to date on their vaccinations,

Not welfare supplicants
But conservative Republicans.
As for these Chinese characters on my forehead,
I had no idea what they said—
They're tattoos—
I got them at the naval station in Newport News
Where I was based.
I was shit-faced
And my buddy Bud Johnson
Dared me to have it done
And thanks to this debility
I work in a federal corrections facility
As a guard
Because I've been scarred
By this unsightly facial feature
And lost my job as a teacher.
It's strange, I know,
But what I've said is so,
I swear on the Bible, Quran, Talmud, and the sacred texts of Tao.
May I board now?

Two Stories

Joe has a Harvard B.A., which everybody wants,
But he's making lattes and warming up croissants
At a ritzy coffee shop for CEOs and their buddies
But this guy majored in women's studies.
He's got the over-educated underpaid barista blues.

He's living with four roommates in a three-room duplex;
He's got no car, no privacy, no sex.
All he has is a futon and a beanbag chair,
A bookcase, an iPad, and plastic dinnerware.

He studied women's lit and wrote his thesis
On Veronica Geng and her *New Yorker* pieces,
But he doesn't have a girlfriend. He's four feet tall
And women don't go for men that small.

He plays in a band called Electric Death Trap.
It's hardcore gangsta jerkin' snap rap.
He dances, sings, he's the star of the show,
And the fans are people he'd never want to know.

His friends are getting married and making a home.
He's making lattes with hearts in the foam.
He's working on an album called *Set Me On Fire*
In hopes he can buy himself a washer and dryer.

It's hard to be different and don't I know it:
Here I am, an unpublished poet.
I write funny, people want pessimistic.
They think cynicism is more artistic.

But my dad invented the circuits of *Delete*
So here I am on West Easy Street,
In a six-bedroom suite at the Ritz Hotel,
Which shows it pays to choose your parents well.

This book *Brisk Verse* has sold fifty-two copies.
Poetry's one of my numerous hobbies.
I'm a painter, pianist, bagpiper, potter,
I love the pitter-patter of raindrops on water.
My poems are pointless but that doesn't matter:
You get the picture? I'm mad as a hatter.
Joe Blow the Harvard barista is wiser
But I have eyes in my upper right incisor
And I can see that it pays to have luck:
You can't be a swan if your dad was a duck.
If your dad is a dodo, then declare you're an orphan,
Be famous, fabulous, take endorphins for more fun.
Be like me, a yachtsman who sails across life's stormy sea,
Who's got lots of pots of the old do-re-mi.
So you ask, why am I in this room at Bellevue?
I'm here in disguise as rich people do
And avoiding attention 'cause you never know who—
The CIA or Internal Revenue—
May out of the blue try to get into
Your riches and pull a switcheroo
And you fall from a penthouse on Park Avenue
To a bench on the edge of Central Park Zoo
And the Unitarian soup kitchen queue,
It's happened to plenty of people I knew,
But enough about me. What's happening with you?

At the Society of Light Verse Annual Banquet

I went to the banquet to get my award,
Wearing a suit I could barely afford,
Surrounded by women in low-cut gowns;
I tried to avert but I kept looking down.

I sat down front close to the aisle,
And prepared my modest but grateful smile,
And thought of what and whom to include
In my humble speech of gratitude.

When the emcee came out with the big envelope,
I drew a deep breath of desperate hope.
I said, "Lord, I have just one plea, which is
Give it to me and not those sons of bitches."

He opened the envelope, and I don't know why
But he read off the name of the wrong guy.
I was gracious about it, I clapped and woo-hooed
But I knew that the fix was in. I'd been screwed.

The winner came sashaying by, what a joke.
I wished he'd collapse from a humongous stroke.
This fatuous talentless ignorant poet.
Oh, for some fresh horse manure—I'd throw it.

The poetry business is corrupt as can be.
It's no place for sensitive artists like me.
The cheating, the bribery, it's cheap and debasing.
That's why I've gone into stock car racing.

I drive a souped-up '56 Oldsmobile,
Three-fifty horsepower, and me at the wheel.
They call me The Avenger and admire my bravado.
I tear up dirt tracks from Illinois to Colorado.
Got a house full of trophies, platinum, gold,
Because in racing, if the truth be told,
Unlike in poetry, where mediocrities shine,
The winner is the one who first crossed the line.

Mr. Freak

Beautiful women in tank tops,
Tall and lean, my jaw drops:
Stop staring or she'll call the cops.
Models out of magazines:
How did they squeeze into those jeans?
A woman with a pair of boobs
That wreaks havoc with my pubes:
If I should look her in the eye,
I can kiss my life goodbye:
Doing time in Leavenworth, Kansas,
8–10 for unwelcome glances
Plus as much as
15–20 for unwanted touches.
A man tempted by adventure,
He could spend the rest of the century
In a penitentiary.
So, for fear my eyes may roam,
I stay at home,
Lock the door and pull the blinds,
Avoiding girls' suspicious minds.
Sometimes, overcome by lust,
Disgusting thoughts that happen just
Because of words I saw
Such as bravado or algebra,
Zebra, candelabra, Brava,
I drop in at a tattoo shop
And have another nude
Woman tattooed

On my skin
In redemption for my sin.
It works. A few episodic
Fits of erotic
Longing occur
But as the tattoos blur
And turn to gray,
Lust fades away,
Just as I shall someday.
Meanwhile I'm the Tattooed Man
In the freak show caravan
On display inside the tent,
A man who underwent torment
To torpedo his libido,
Which it has done:
Look at me, son.
Thanks to the injections
Of dye, I
Have no erections,
Not one.

TOMATO BLUES

I planted tomatoes in my garden
In the warm wet ground,
Now I've got the blues 'cause my tomatoes are turning brown.

The tomatoes in supermarkets
Taste like Styrofoam.
So I went to the trouble of planting tomatoes at home.

I planted Big Boys, my neighbor planted Brandywine.
He has two rows of tomatoes, all doing fine.
His are being harvested, mine are dying on the vine.

My neighbor's an idiot, a racist, and a jerk,
His politics are right-wing bordering on berserk.
I mulch and water my tomatoes and nothing seems to work.

So one night at 3 a.m. I tiptoed next door.
I pissed on his tomatoes and then pissed some more.
And the next morning looked and they were redder than before.
I tossed seeds by his tomatoes to attract the blackbirds.
But they descended on mine, herds of blackbirds,
Ate my tomatoes and left piles of blackbird turds.

There's no justice in this world, of this I'm sure.
Fortune smiles on the corrupt and frowns upon the pure.
I planted beautiful tomatoes and I harvested manure.

May Snow

In Minnesota, we don't count on spring in April,
We have a climate of diversity.
It's possible that a May morning's paper'll
Say, "Snow expected tomorrow or Thursday."

We do not complain, we simply say,
"Welcome to Minnesota" and march forth.
Snow in May, but we are pretty much okay.
And pretty much okay is good enough here in the North.

If it snows in May, we do not fuss about our misery,
Whimper, make a stink or whinge or cry,
For everyone else is in the same boat as we,
And soon the sun will shine, if not in June, July.
And when the crocuses come up, the tulips, and the purple gentian,
We feel joy, though it's nothing we'd ever mention.

Haydn Piano Sonata

Here I am, I'm in my seat.
Shoes are polished, clothes are neat,
At the concert hall to hear
Haydn's opus for klavier.

When I hear someone behind,
Someone very unrefined
Rustling their program page,
And I turn in rage: HEY

Beat it, stupid, go get lost or I will
Shove that program up your nostril.
I am listening to this work.
Where were you brought up? A barn? You jerk.

Sweet and graceful, light and clear,
Haydn falling on my ear,
Perfect order, perfect grace,
Every note is in its place.

Then somebody to the right
Turns in loudly for the night
And I wait for one loud note
So I can cut his throat. (SLICE)

Serves him right, the little creep, he
Should've gone back home if he was sleepy.
I just hope his blood won't drip
Distracting from the great musicianship.

I would gladly put your feet
In a bucket of concrete,
Find a bridge to drop you off,
If you don't stop that cough. (BAM)

If your coughing doesn't clear up,
I will put a drug in your cough syrup.
Music is a gift from God,
Please shut up and at the end, applaud.

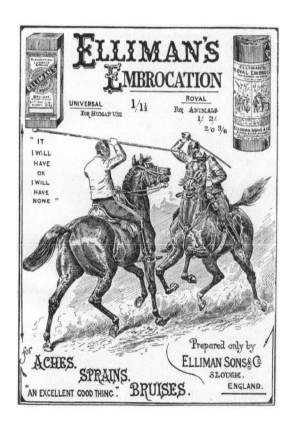

UNFINISHED MELODY

It was Friday afternoon when I wrote this song,
It's Saturday now but it won't be for long.
On Sunday I leave town
And the leaves that are green turn brown.
I wrote this song for a girl named Eileen
But she was with her friends
And the leaves that were green
Turn brown as summer ends.
Love comes and goes away
Like so many other things
And a man sings his song
And then sees that his audience is gone.

I rode an elevator to the fifth floor
And then I rode it back down.
It was a men's clothing store
And they didn't have green pants, just brown.
Once I wrote better songs than this,
Everybody said they were
Profound,
But after I lost her
My good songs turned to brown.
They are blowing in the wind,
A meaningless noun
No more to be seen
What once was green.

T. S.

Let's ditch T.S. Eliot, baby, bid him goodbye
When the evening is spread out against the sky,
Him and his half-deserted streets and cheap hotels,
The smoke in sawdust restaurants with oyster shells.
Instead of writing poetry, he should've stuffed a sock
In his mouth and forgot about J. Alfred Prufrock
And the Waste Land with all of its debris
And called up Information and got in touch with Marie.
She was a peach. She could've gotten his trousers rolled,
Could've gotten them off, got him in a good hold,
Let him hear the mermaids singing in the sea,
Sing away his lonely nights in Memphis, Tennessee.
    If T.S. had eased Marie out of her bra and girdle,
      The Waste Land could've been quite green and fertile.

Appleton

On the vernal equinox young people walk along the Fox River
    on Wisconsin State 29,
Birds perched on the powerline,
Cows stand in the field and chew
And do the things that cattle do.
Horses and buggies here and there,
A smell of skunk in the air.
And then Appleton is near
And they smell beer.

There on College Street is an ugly statue
Like a phallus coming at you.
And in the vicinity
The outposts of masculinity
Where men pursue a career
In beer. Day and night,
Budweiser, Schlitz, Miller Lite,
And for the frugal,
Leinenkugel.

Bars as far as you can see
Where you can drink and pee.
Cleo's, Jim's Place, The Déjà Vu.
The Ultra Lounge, Drinks Inc., and The Bar on the Avenue.
Señor Tequila's, Shark's Billiards Bar and Grill
Where beautiful young people will
Ignore the good advice of their mother
And consort with each other

Bopping along in T-shirts,
Jackets open, girls in short skirts,
And you're dancing with a guy you met
Smoking a hand-rolled cigarette,
Feeling good on some stuff you sniffed,
Getting down on Taylor Swift
Singing about escaping
Bad boyfriends and you're vaping,
The room is spinning around
Your mouth tastes of sweeping compound,
You're dizzy and rotten
In the arms of someone whose name you've forgotten,
Maybe it's Jim, maybe Joe,
And he says, "Let's go"
And doesn't say where
And you don't care.
You feel life is a beautiful buffet
In Appleton, Wisconsin, U.S.A.
But eventually it's Monday,
He's gone away down the highway,
There's a bill to pay
Here at the Holiday
Inn in Monterey,
California.
We tried to warn you.
Oh, Laura,
Like Pandora
You opened a big box
When you left the Fox.
He messed up your mind,
Left you behind,

Your Visa card's been declined,

And you called me, your old boss at the Appleton Coffee Grind,

And you said, "Jack,

Can I have my old job back,

And an advance on my salary?"

But I've already hired your sister Mallory

And she's a gem, truly extraordinary, and so sweet,

But here's $100 to help you get back on your feet.

Have a nice day.

Have you considered A.A.?

TIME TO LEAVE TOWN

We're going down to the other end of town, kid,
And see if the party's down there.
They invited your sister. What's with her?
She's not cool. I thought we were.
We stream on Nolo, we text on Jam.
We're the only ones in this town to know about BioFam.
Your sister doesn't have IsaBell or use DuoPhones.
I'm sure she still listens to the Rolling Stones.
She's out to lunch, she missed the bus.
So why did they invite her and not us?

We wrote the book about zero-sum history.
Others were puzzled, we solved the mystery.
AI, CP, LSMFT,
We're all over it, you and me.
They didn't invite us to their soirée.
They're probably eating burgers and listening to Beyoncé.
Your sister is so Seventies and her hair is silver gray,
That platinum-plated silver that is utterly passé.
Maybe it's time we left Minneapolis and moved to L.A.
What do you say?

MAN'S FALL

My cellphone's almost dead;
Power's down to half a bar.
She's on her way, so she said,
To pick me up in her car.
I gave her my address
But she doesn't have GPS.
She could be nearby
Trying to call.
I could just cry.
Not just cry, bawl.
Wait. A message. *Access denied.*
Password unidentified.
Sorry for the inconvenience.
Press CONTINUE to report your grievance.
I've been working on seduction,
Trying to get her to the chapel,
And now this malfunction.
Call me Adam. I'm screwed by Apple.

COFFEE

I used to love plain coffee, black and hot,
Now my coffee costs eight bucks a shot.
The man makes me one and I can't refuse.
I got them espresso blues.

He grinds dark beans from Brazil.
He froths up the milk and grinds up daffodil.
He flips the switch and my espresso drips.
Can't wait to bring the cup to my lips.

I take a taste and it burns my tongue.
Like me, it's bitter and rather high-strung.
He makes me another. Is it crazy? I guess so.
I sure do love my morning espresso.

I'm late with the rent, and my car broke down.
I owe money to people all over this town.
Got no friends. My social life sucks.
All I have is this Starbucks.

Set 'em up, Joe. One more cup.
I need to get caffeined up.
No gin or wine, no soda, no tea,
Just a coffee dependency.

My girlfriend left me 'cause I'm so wired.
She looks at me and it makes her tired.
I talk so fast, it sounds absurd.
Nerves are on edge, my vision is blurred.

I'm sleepless, can't lie down and rest.
I'm irritable 'cause I'm over-espressed.
The phone rings, it makes me jump.
I started to think I might vote for Trump.
That's when I gave up self-abuse
And I switched over to apple juice.

4. DEVOTIONAL

CHRISTMAS

While shepherds texted on their phones
A night so dark and cold,
The angels of the Lord came down
And put them all on Hold.

And the angels told the Wise Men
Who came from faraway.
And the shepherds heard the message on
Voicemail the next day.

"The child is in a manger
Among the cows and sheep.
Rise up and sing, and come and see,
And behold him in the (BEEP)."

They found the spot with GPS
And saw the bright star shine
And took a selfie with the child
And posted it online.

And the shepherds surfed awhile
To see what they could see.
And the child in the manger lay
Waiting patiently.

And He is waiting still today
After His Ascension.
So set your phone aside, I pray,
And look up at the Milky Way,
Sit and pay attention.

Only for You

The night you came into the world
In the dark, my little girl,
Venturing out alone,
Your arms waved and your dark eyes shone.
Your tiny body did a dance
As I took you in my hands.

There were times at 3 a.m.
You created such mayhem,
Your daddy walked the floor with you,
Sang all the lullabies he knew.
I tried a drop of Benadryl,
Felt guilty about that, but still,
You fell asleep. I lay awake
Listening for each breath you'd take.

One night at a restaurant,
Green pesto sauce you seemed to want,
Two calamari chunks you took,
And then gave me a funny look.
I made my hands into a cup
And what went down came right back up.
You're the only one I'd do that for.
It only made me love you more.

I changed your diaper one day
And you stood and walked away.
I looked up and saw you run
And realized that you weren't done.
I caught it before it hit the floor;
You're the only one I'd do that for.

Jesus said, "Children, come unto me."
Except we become as children, we
Can't enter the blessed eternity.
As I get old, again and again,
Instead of 80 I'm eight or ten,
Maybe stumble, start weeping too,
Make a mess, need help from you.
And I will fly away, my love,
And follow you from up above.

SCHOOL BUSES

Out on the prairie so wide
The school buses wending their way.
From the towns they travel
For miles on the gravel
An hour before it is day.
And the winter wind blows
'Cross the corn stubble rows
Where the dirt has turned the snow gray.

And the kids think of math as they go
And the meaning of a light year
And unequal equations
And verb conjugations
And the sonnets of William Shakespeare.
And then up the drive
At the school they arrive
On the darkest day of the year.

In a few years they will fly
Away, young women and men
With mixed emotions
'Cross mountains and oceans
And become what we could not have been.
We will tenderly kiss them
Goodbye and miss them,
They will write to us now and then
As they spread their wings
And do noble things,
Taking notes with paper and pen,
They'll create, they'll heal,
And deal with what's real,
And we never will see them again.

TEACHERS

Pearson, Hochstetter, Bradley, and Shaver,
Anderson, Story, Moehlenbrock, Faust,
Names I remember for their great kindness
Decades ago in a country schoolhouse.

Moehlenbrock, Pearson, Shaver, and Story,
Anderson, Faust, Hochstetter, and Bradley
Stand by the blackboard in memory's classroom
I hear their voices and think of them gladly.

Shaver, Anderson, Bradley, and Story,
Pearson, Moehlenbrock, Faust, Hochstetter,
Public school teachers, back in my childhood,
Would that I could write them all a love letter.

I was that slight insignificant child,
A B-minus student and painfully shy,
The wire-rimmed glasses, the hand-me-down clothing.
Why do I think of you as time goes by?

Nothing you do for a child is wasted.
Kindness, scholarship, letters, and love.
I sat in the back and looked at the blackboard,
Lincoln and Washington hanging above.

It was only a schoolhouse out in the country,
A high school in a small river town.
But Shakespeare, physics, the owl's bone structure,
Equations, and books, books all around.
Anderson, Hochstetter, Shaver, and Pearson,
Moehlenbrock, Faust, Bradley and Story.
Decades have passed but I see their bright faces
There in the classroom, shining in glory.

Shining in glory, shining in glory,
Your blessed teachers, they shine every one
Always remembered for what they have done,
Always remembered for what they have done.

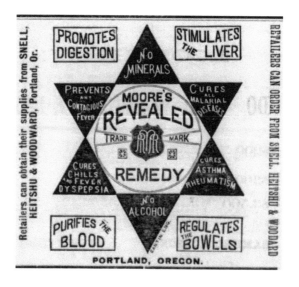

Norma Jean

A long time ago, a girl Norma Jean
Became a model at the age of 18
And appeared nude in a magazine,
Which made her famous and led to the screen
And she turned into Marilyn Monroe.

She married a baseball hero named Joe
Who was jealous and he didn't know
How hard it would be to be walking with
A beautiful blond American myth.

She made some good movies such as *Bus Stop*,
Comedies like *Some Like It Hot*,
Married Arthur Miller, a serious writer,
And for a time, life became brighter.
She threw herself into the marriage,
Had psychotherapy, had a miscarriage,
She worked at being a real actress,
Not just let the wind blow up her dress,
But she developed an appetite
For drugs to get her through the night.

She died alone in the Hollywood Hills,
Went to bed with bottles of pills,
And in the dark, in depression and fear,
Decided she'd rather no longer be here.
Poor Norma Jean,
We didn't mean to be such a weight,
We were only out to celebrate
Love and life and glamor,
Not be a sledgehammer.
We repent of making you into an allegory,
Adulation turned crematory,
Your very name, *memento mori*.
Rest in peace and rise in glory.

Mozart

When Mozart was three, he began to play the clavier.
At five, he started to compose;
When he was ten, already launched on his career,
He began to worry about his hair and clothes.
"This silk shirtwaist," he wondered. "Does it emphasize my slender figure?
Is my hair too light? Should I dye it brunet?
Do these embroidered britches make my butt look bigger?
Will people laugh at my new string quartet?"
Even a genius is full of doubts.
Should the third movement be in 4/4 rhythm?
How will he look in silver breechclouts?
After the concert, will the Duke want to dine with him?

Thank you, Mozart, for being so brilliant and prolific.
And by the way, your hair looks really terrific.

JOANNE

Blest be the woman in white.
I lie and look up at her
Who holds my hand to take my pulse
And also my temperature.

In the hum of the I.C.U.
Amid the machines she stands.
Amid all the technology I feel
The laying on of hands.

She asks me how I feel.
I tell her, "Much better today."
Now that the tube is out of my throat
And the catheter's gone away.

I came here for heart surgery
To repair my right atrium.
And now we're discussing the weather forecast,
They say there's more snow to come.

My life has been handed back to me
And what is so dear to my heart
Is the sound of her Midwestern voice
As she writes on my patient chart.

The mystery of life is here
Of life and death and man
And also the human kindness
Of an angel named Joanne.

Freddy Keillor, R.I.P.

My grandson Frederick, young Freddy,
Was bright and kept pressing ahead, he
Studied Chinese,
Knew hundreds of trees,
Tossed out facts like confetti.

He knew everything about cars,
The bugs he collected in jars.
A boy of ambition,
He left on a mission
To visit the planets and stars.

He never meant, God forbid,
To cause the grief that he did.
He meant to go high
And fly to the sky
And return as a well-traveled kid.

We think of him out there at play
In a cosmos of permanent day.
Still in existence
Though at a distance,
Turning and learning
All things concerning
Wonder and wisdom,
The solar system,
Planets and particles,
Magazine articles,
Taking delight
In hearing and sight,
Constantly keen
And forever sixteen,
Getting farther and farther away.

Our Old Cat

On Friday she was not herself at all.
She lay, face turned to the wall,
Silent and subdued,
And did not touch her food.
On Sunday she didn't purr
When we petted her
And she seemed far away.
We knelt by the bed where she lay
And felt desolate and sad
And told her, "Good cat, good cat,"
And then this delicate creature
Of an affectionate nature
Had to be carried outside
And taken for a ride
To the vet who with gentle affection
Administered the merciful injection
As we stroked her and said,
"Good cat. Good cat." And she laid down her head
On our lap
And took her nap.

It's childish, to feel such grief
For an animal whose life is brief.
And if it's foolish, so it be.
She was good company,
And we miss that gift
Of cat affection while she lived.
Beauty is beauty: and that's
The reason God created cats.

EPISCOPAL ROUSER

I'm slow to anger, don't covet or lust.
No sins of pride except sometimes I really must.

Episcopalian, giving my love to you.
The theology's easy, the liturgy too.
Just stand up and kneel down and do what the others do.
Episcopalian, and tasteful of course, through and through.

We're not Catholics, don't take our complaints
And kneel down and pray to the statues of saints.
Nor are we Baptists, our rectors don't tell
Us all the ways we might go to hell.
At St. Michael's, we recycle,
At St. Clement's, it's gin and lemons.
Morning dawns on great white swans
On the lawns of St. John's.
There's white folks and black, and gay and morose,
Some old fundamentalists but we watch them pretty close.
No matter whom, you're good, we assume.
Episcopalian, saving our love for you.

LUTHERAN CREDO

I'm from Minneapolis, south Minneapolis,
Lived there all my life.
When I die I'll be buried in Lakewood,
Right alongside my wife.
We are members of Central Lutheran,
Fifty years, same pew.
I like the folks who sit back there
They're Norwegian too.

Lutherans are modest people,
We're great at humility,
And it sure would be a better world
If they were all as modest as we.
We sing the hymns, listen to the sermon,
Go up front and commune.
Drop in the money, shake hands with the pastor,
And we're out by a quarter to noon.

Episcopalians are proud of their faith,
You ought to hear them talk.
Who they got? They got Henry the 8th
And we got J.S. Bach.
Henry the 8th'd marry a woman
And then her head would drop.
J.S. Bach had 23 kids
'Cause his organ had no stop.

If you come to church, don't expect to be hugged,
Don't expect your hand to be shook.
If we need to know who the heck you are,
We can look in the visitors' book.
I was raised to keep a lid on it,
Guard what you say or do.
A Mighty Fortress is our God
So he must be Lutheran too.

Our pastor is not that bad,
Preaches Scripture chapter and verse.
He's better than others we've had,
And I tell you, I've heard a lot worse.
We avoid pride and falsehood,
And the choir sings pretty well.
We do our best to do good.
So we're Lutheran, what the hell.

JEAN

She boarded a plane and flew to Denver;
She has back pains and won't complain ever.
She walks all bent over at 91.
But her sister died and there's work to be done.

She'll spend a month in Colorado,
Bury her sister and clean out the condo
And care for her niece who's autistic, Marie,
And figure out where Marie needs to be.

She's 91 and her sister is dead,
There's a funeral to arrange and words to be said.
A will to probate and a condo to sell
And a girl who cannot care for herself.

Since she was a child on the farm, she knew it:
There's work to be done, so you step up and do it.
You clean and you cook and you do what is right
So she's off to Denver on the afternoon flight.

In every family there's someone like Jean.
When there's a crisis, she heads for the scene.
Making her way and she'll find what she finds,
Going about things with a practical mind.

Laundry, groceries, clean up the mess.
Bring calm and order to a scene of distress.
Call up her brother, call the funeral home,
Promise Marie she won't be left alone.
That old lady you see in line at the gate.
Say a prayer for her as you wait.
May the Almighty keep her in His care.
She is needed by someone and she's heading there.

They Were So Young

Memorial Day and the old folks come
And stand in the sun feeling sad and dumb.
The boys in the ground—there are so many,
They're eighteen, nineteen, maybe twenty—
They just moved out of a boy's bedroom
And went to war, now they lie in a tomb.
Old people come on Memorial Day
And people speak but what's there to say?
The dead would trade it all for the chance
To find a girl and ask her to dance.

Ticonderoga, Hamburger Hill,
Young men marching out to kill.
Manassas, Shiloh, Chancellorsville,
They fell down and they lie there still.

World War I: they picked up their arms
And marched to Ypres and the Battle of the Marne
Vimy Ridge, Passchendaele, the Somme,
Midwestern boys far from home.
Iwo Jima and Normandy,
Anzio and the Coral Sea,
The Battle of the Bulge, the Korean War,
Pork Chop Hill, the Chosin Reservoir,
Loc Ninh, Dak To, the siege of Khe Sanh,
The Tet Offensive and the battle of Saigon:
Young men running and young men fall,
Their names are inscribed on a long stone wall.

Iraq, Afghanistan, again and again,
The story repeated of elderly men
Wary of appearing weak,
Needing heroic lines to speak,
Sent the young men out to die,
Leaving the mothers and sisters to cry.
Bells are rung, hymns are sung,
Flowers are brought and strewed among,
But it breaks your heart:
They were so young.
They died so young.

PRAYER

Here I am, O Lord, and here is my prayer:
Please be there.
Don't want to ask too much, miracles and such.
Just whisper in the air: please be there.
When I die like other folks,
Don't want to find out You're a hoax.
I'm not on my knees asking for world peace
Or that the polar icecap freeze
And save the polar bear
Or even that the poor be fed
Or angels hover o'er my bed
But I will sure be pissed
If I should have been an atheist.
Lord, please exist. Thou
Before Whom I bow,
Come to me now.

CHRISTMAS

A little girl is singing for the faithful to come ye
Joyful and triumphant, a song that means
A cheerful houseful of children and family
And food and bright lights in fresh greens,
Red lights and silver and bright blue
Where the faithful live, some joyful, some troubled,
Enduring old age and symptoms of the flu,
While fighting clutter and keeping the sidewalk shoveled.
Not much triumph going on here—and yet
There is much we do not understand.
And my hopes and fears are met
In this small singer holding onto my hand.
      Onward we go, faithful, hopeful, into the dark,
      And are there angels hovering overhead? Hark.

ANGEL

To Mary D. Kierstead

I want to thank you, darling, that back in 1969,
Looking through a pile of unsolicited stories at *The New Yorker*, you
pulled out mine
And sent it to an editor and said, "Read it,"
Which was what I desperately needed.

I imagine you, a graduate of Barnard, a writer yourself,
Working through piles of paper on a shelf,
An angel smoking a menthol cigarette,
Horn-rimmed glasses, hair the color of sunset,
Hundreds of writers hoping to catch a ride
And the importance of angels cannot be denied.

Fifty years have passed since I made you smile
But to me it's still happening, my story in the pile.
If you choose me I'll write books and do a radio show
And marry Jenny. And if you don't, I don't know.
I'll sit in a parking lot shack, a pint of bourbon in my coat,
Grieving for all the stories that I never wrote.

You chose me and it led me to a better place.
Fifty years illuminated by your grace.
I write this poem, my dear, and lay it at your feet,
My angelic first reader at 25 West 43rd Street.

STEPHANIE

My editor Stephanie Beck,
Spectacles hung round her neck,
Slowly goes through
With a sharp No. 2
To review and to check and recheck.
She crosses out "that" and writes "which,"
Changes "corner" to "niche."
Like a marshal on TV,
The tireless Stevie
Is the law, and I love her, the bitch.

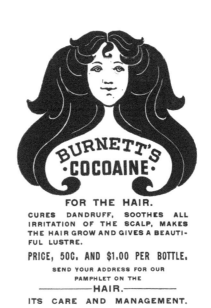

FOR THE HAIR.

CURES DANDRUFF, SOOTHES ALL IRRITATION OF THE SCALP, MAKES THE HAIR GROW AND GIVES A BEAUTIFUL LUSTRE.

PRICE, 50C. AND $1.00 PER BOTTLE.

SEND YOUR ADDRESS FOR OUR PAMPHLET ON THE
———————HAIR.———————
ITS CARE AND MANAGEMENT.

Joseph Burnett Co., Boston.

Hymn to My Homeland

I've traveled all over this country,
From New York to the tall redwood trees.
I even spent two days in Texas
Don't ask me what happened there, please.
I visited every mountain range,
All the coasts, and was unimpressed
Until I drove across the plains
And discovered the Upper Midwest.

The landscape is gentle and fertile,
The prairie is pure paradise,
There are people named Elmer and Myrtle,
And everyone talks to you nice.

The springtime is flower and blossom,
And summer's not bad on the whole,
The autumn is golden and awesome,
And winter is good for your soul.

The bluebirds and meadowlarks winging
Comfort us with melody,
And thanks to our Christian upbringing
We sing in four-part harmony.

We're taught to take turns and speak slowly
And share and not lay up treasure,
And that politeness is holy,
So we say "please" and "my pleasure."

We were brought up on the Bible
To be modest and harmonious.
So when it comes to the tribal
There's no tribe nicer than us.

The Stars and Stripes Forever

Now is the time for all good men
To celebrate democracy
From the shores of Waikiki
To the streets of New York City.

The nation of the brave and true,
Of comedy and whoop-de-doo
And birch canoes and lobster stew
And the humble hot dog too.

It's a nation of splendor and pizzazz
And boffo lollapalooza
Of hullabaloo and razzmatazz
All expressed by John Philip Sousa.

    Hurrah for the Stars and the Stripes
    And for polka dots and plaids and for zigzag,
    For the red and the white and the blue
    And also for tasteful pastels.

    Hurrah for the U.S. of A.
    Tuscaloosa, Honolulu, and Utah,
    Seattle, San Francisco, and St. Paul,
    Albuquerque, Abilene, Apache Junction.

Here's to Unitarians,
Union members, supervisors,
Schoolteachers, social workers,
Auditors, assistants, actors,

The farmers who plow the ground,
The pilots flying in the air,
The cops and guards who look around
To keep us on the square.

It's a nation of big football games
And bands marching into the stadium,
And art shows with paintings in frames,
And weddings with brides looking radiant.

Hurrah for the Stars and the Stripes
And for ovals, triangles, and circles,
Rectangles of every kind
And also parallelograms.
Happy Fourth of July to our friends
And our deluded opponents.
Today is a day to join hands
And let us sing about the Stars and Stripes Forever.
BOOM.

Mormon

Was Ethel Merman a Mormon?
And how about Jessye Norman?
General Sherman or Uma Thurman:
Mormon? Or German?
In an enormous auditorium
The former Mormons stood
Performing "Stormy Weather"
As warmly as they could.
I'm not a Mormon, nor are you
Neither was Harmon Killebrew.
The Little Mermaid used to be;
She murmured mournfully to me.

Standing nearer to a mirror,
Did Norma Shearer see a Mormon?
Norman Mailer? New York doormen?
Carmen Miranda? Marine Corps men?
Jury foremen? Or longshoremen?
A dorm of sophomore men?
Larry, Curly, Shemp, and Moe?
Marilyn Monroe? We do not know.

5. GUYS

FATHERHOOD

Human sperm are very small,
Five microns, that's about all.
They're just a cell with a dangly tail.
A fraction of the ovum,
But still you've got to love 'em
And they're produced in the testes of the male.
Beneath their shiny domes
They contain your chromosomes
And the tail can kick just like a leg.
O nothing could be fina
Than to swim up a vagina
In search of a rendezvous with an egg.

The sperm has one ambition
And that's to gain admission
To the female reproductive canal.
And once he gets in it
He swims a millimeter a minute
Along with forty million of his pals.
The sperm is no boob,
When he smells the Fallopian tube
He goes into some crazy figure eights
About ten thousand times
As those female enzymes
Keep egging him on to penetrate.
A few sperm advance
And do their little dance,

But only one gets through the egg membrane,
And the merger of those two—
That's what led to you
So be thankful that your folks did not abstain.

That old man in the garage
Once let loose a great barrage
And though he now is ancient and infirm
And his breath is bad—
Children, he's your dad
Because he contributed those sperm.

You can get it from a bank
Or from Jim or John or Frank
But when it comes to fatherhood there's just one guy to thank.
He was young and he was dumb
But when things began to hum,
He did not withdraw,
He became our pa
And that is where each one of us came from.

OPERA

Why is it that, in Rossini and Verdi,
Entertainment is such a rarity?
Verdi's *Aida*
Goes on for hours.
You need a double margarita
And two whiskey sours
And a double martini
For Puccini.
Rigoletto: by the time it's through
And Gilda's in the bag, I wish I were too.
Don Pasquale is not so jolly.
Strauss's *Ariadne* is pure monotony.
I sat and yawned through *Pélleas and Mélisande.*
And Benjamin Britten
Wrote the most boring music ever written.
And Mussorgsky was modest, of course,
Because his operas were not Godunov, so they Boris.

The *Ring of the Nibelungs*
With all of those goddesses,
The braids and the bodices—
If they had more feeble lungs,
Brunhilde and her crowd
Wouldn't sing so loud.
Like someone's been floggin' her,
Someone like Wagner.

My love loves opera with a love strong and pure
So I go along with it and sit next to her.
And as the opera soars from tragedy to sublimity,
I simply enjoy her proximity.
I am impervious to gloom.
I'd be happily buried in a tomb
Like Radamès,
Anonymous and incognita,
If she were my Aida.

At the Clinic

I'm trying to bring forth some urine
At a medical clinic, secure in
Knowing I've peed
Whenever I need-
Ed, so help me Martin Van Buren.
Just pee in the cup
About halfway up
For a lab technician to stir in
Some little dye
To indicate that I
Have cancer for which there's no cure. In
Silence I stand,
Gadget in hand,
And think of my true love and her in
The room where they wait.
I urinate,
The test's negative,
So I shall live
And take her to Naples and Turin.
Off we shall go
And she'll never know
The tragedy we almost were in.

The Wreck of My Old 97

I had an appointment at the Mayo Clinic
To have me an MRI.
It was on a cold cold day in November
Under a cloudy sky.

I had my '97 Chevy aimed at Rochester
South on 52
With a full tank of gas and the radio playing
And the tires were all brand-new.

I was goin' down the road making sixty miles an hour,
Listening to the radio.
It was Bill Monroe playing old-time bluegrass
And he did not play it slow.

I was near Zumbrota, following a semi,
When a deer jumped into the gap.
I hit the brakes and I swerved toward the shoulder
And my coffee fell into my lap.

In my shock I threw the car into Park
And I heard the transmission scream
And the crankshaft fell out on the highway.
It was all like a real bad dream.

It blew the front tires and I skidded in the ditch
For I could no longer steer;
In the back seat, I was carrying an anvil
And it flew right past my ear.

And the airbag opened as my car flipped over,
Ten times it cartwheeled
Through the trees with the engine smoking
And it came to rest in a field.

I leaped from the wreck and I dove for cover
And I heard that gas tank blow.
The flames leaped up in a giant conflagration
To the music of Bill Monroe.

The radio played as the flames leaped higher,
You could hear the fiddle cry.
It played "Will the Circle Be Unbroken,
By and by, Lord, by and by."

The radio played as the car burned to ashes
And the tires and frame were gone.
You can wreck your car until it's a ruin
But Bill Monroe goes on.

The deer escaped and the semi kept trucking
And they took that MRI,
A picture of my brain and it was all in order
And responding to stimuli.

Ever since that day I have watched for deer
And I'm grateful, praise the Lord,
And I don't carry anvils in the back seat
Or coffee on my dashboard.

GRANDSONS

In the backyard here you be
Sitting on your grandpa's knee,
Freddy and his brother Charlie
Eating chocolate candy.

Summer days when I was a kid
All the funny things we did
When grown-ups came, we ran and hid
Back behind the lilacs.

Back when I was ten years old,
Rode my bike on dusty roads
Through the fields of corn and oats
Pretending it was a Harley.

In the heat of the summer sun
Round and round the yard we run,
Chased the dog and just for fun
We put him in the sprinkler.

Tearing all around the place
Through the woods and home we chase,
Capture the Flag and Prisoner's Base
Until we're called for supper.

Summer days my pals and I
Lay and looked up at the sky
Hoping someday we could fly
Over Minnesota.

Back when I was young as you,
I fought with the boys in blue
Chasing Stonewall Jackson through
The valleys of Virginia.

Then I joined the ranks of men
Never to be free again,
Drive away down Highway 10
Heading for the office.

But now and then I break away.
A child climbs on me, I neigh
And whinny as I eat the hay
As he slaps me on the hinder.

Fathers and Sons

My father had a lot to tell me,
Things I ought to know,
Mistakes not to make,
Rules not to break.
But then I left home to find out on my own
And I know my father knew:
There's only so much you can do.

You're proud when they walk,
Scared when they run.
That's how it is
Between fathers and sons.

It's a bridge you can't cross,
A cross you can't bear.
Things you can't change
No matter how much you care.

Mothers try to protect you
But a kid will get free
And the farther you go
The more you can see.
And there's nothing to say
Except "Find your own way."
You do what you can
But you have to let go.
You're just part of the flow
Of the river that runs
Between fathers and sons.

PANTOMIME

The farmer walked in his orchard green
Where he would surely not be seen
For he felt a need he could not dismiss,
The simple need to take a piss.
His shepherd dog stood by his side
As he unzipped his trousers wide,
Pulled out his manhood and released
A golden stream like any beast.
From a maple limb an old magpie
Looked down on him with an evil eye
As he happily took his leak,
The magpie gave a terrible shriek,
The dog he barked and the magpie crapped
And the farmer yelled and something snapped
And he tried to zip his trousers up
And accidentally kicked the pup
Who bit the farmer in the butt
And he zipped the zipper shut
Not noticing that his balls
Were not within his overalls
And so the zipper one ball snipped
And in his pain the farmer tripped
And staggered in a sort of dance
In great distress and shit his pants.
The dog looked at him in dismay
And the magpie laughed and flew away.

GREENSLEEVES

He wore a shirt that was made of leaves,
A green shirt with long green sleeves,
A leafy shirt seems strange and yet—
A shirt made of tea? Or sweat?
Nor would you ever catch me wearing
A suit made from the bones of herring.
And not with a shirt made from a dress:
It would offend my manliness.
No, sir, no pants of snow for me,
Good jeans are my heredity.
I recall my father said it, he
Said, "A man will do his best
Only if he is properly dressed."
For me that means a suit and vest,
Everything cleaned and pressed,
Black socks and Oxfords on my feet.
Cleanly shaved, hair combed neat,
Greeting strangers in the street,
Reserved but cheerful and upbeat,
With the common touch and yet elite.
That's the man I aim to be,
A paragon of normality.

Memphis Love

Long distance information, give me Memphis, Tennessee,
Someone down at FedEx trying to get in touch with me.
They came here with a package but nobody was home
So they went back to the warehouse and they called us on the phone.

It's a package from my dentist, and it's my lower bridge.
Today is Tuesday and tomorrow she and I'll get hitched.
I bought her the big diamond and a fancy bridal wreath,
But I don't think she'll marry me if I don't get my teeth.

Help me information, and call Federal Express.
If they could meet me at the church, that would be the best.
I'll be in the parking lot, so tell them hurry, please.
My car's the one with tin cans and the windows smeared with cheese.

I'll be looking for the truck, hoping that it comes.
Hoping that my false teeth fit nicely on my gums.
Long distance information, don't hang up on me,
I'm chewing more than I bit off in Memphis, Tennessee.

I got my hair cut yesterday, I'm wearing my new tux,
We're going on a honeymoon that costs two hundred bucks.
Already put the money down, too late to get it back,
And if she were to dump me now I'd have a heart attack.

I am 68 and this is my first romance;
I was very cautious, never dared to take the chance.
She and I love Elvis, pot roast, and Oreos,
And we love to polka, so I ventured to propose.

I'm shaking with excitement as I think of having sex.
So much is depending on this shipment from FedEx.
I'll be in the parking lot and if I see the truck,
I will know there's such a thing as beginner's luck.

Uncle New York

I'm waiting for you here on the Upper West Side.
Whenever you come, we'll take a ride
On the No. 1, you and me, my dear,
To the Met to see *Der Rosenkavalier*.
And after an hour of grand opera passion,
We'll stand in the lobby at intermission
And watch a parade of dazzling fashion
For which people didn't ask their parents' permission.

You come to New York to learn how to live.
And a New York uncle is your favorite relative.
Your father tells you when to stand, when to kneel.
Your uncle tells you to say how you feel.
Your mother says: no pushing, no hitting.
In New York? Ha! Are you kidding?
But don't bring your boyfriend who casts a pall
With his personality like a brick wall,
A pill and a sourpuss, who's always bored.
Darling, you deserve to be adored.
So dump him. Bid him goodbye.
Three is a crowd. It'll be you and I
In our stunning fashion repertoire,
People admiring how cool we are
Strolling around the Central Park Reservoir.
We'll go to La Belle Masque, ask for a corner booth,
And sit on display, objets d'beauty and youth.
Bluepoint oysters and steak tartare
And a glass of wine from the bar.

Go ahead, try that 1978 Merlot,

Thirty bucks a glass is expensive, I know,

But it's worth it. So let's live it up.

Our blessings overrun the cup.

Maybe when we're old and feeble

We'll join the American Association of Cautious People.

But here in New York, we honor our inner child

And embrace the opportunity to be wild

And spread your wings in the metropolitan jungle.

So says your uncle.

We'll be inspired by the lights, the heights of the towers,

Chrysler Building, the Top of the Rock, the Empire State, we'll make them ours.

Everyone should have a New York uncle, be glad that you do.

One who's amused by what is daring and new.

And if you should think big and lose

Your shirt and maybe your shoes

And get the news that the money's gone

And you must give up filet mignon for chicken stew,

Well, remember that the blues is a great American art form too.

The Logger Lover

As I walked out one evening
Into a small café,
A forty-year-old waitress
These words to me did say:
"I'm looking for a lover
Who eats his sirloin rare
And drinks his coffee black
And will touch me here and there.
My lover was a logger
Who never shaved his hide.
He pounded in his whiskers
And chewed them off inside.
A fisherman and hunter
And his name was Rolf
One day he traded his chainsaw
For a club and took up golf.
He became a developer
And wore designer clothes
And started using handkerchiefs
Whenever he blew his nose.
He gave up bootleg whiskey
And took up Chardonnay
And gave up Waylon Jennings
For Gabriel Fauré.
My logger became a jogger
And ran a marathon
And when he gave up snoring,
I told him he was gone."

I said, "If you want a lover.
I'm free and here I stand
And I could learn to cut down trees
And blow my nose by hand."
She said, "You need to be profane
And show your independence
By shouting at the top of your voice
With two f-words in every sentence.
And comb your hair in a ducktail
And hog the middle of the road
And never wipe your rear end
After you dump a load."
I told her, "That's a lot to ask.
I'll give it a shot. Let's see."
She said, "And you must have bad breath
And your verbs and nouns disagree."

So I took up whiskey
And learned to use a hammer
And pound in my whiskers
And even use bad grammar.
I said, "Me and you is very tight,
We could scratch each other's backs
And I would rather be in love
Than use the right syntax."
She said, "There's one more problem.
You must vote for Donald Trump."
I said, "I don't mind ignorance
But I am not a chump.
I don't fall for con men

Who lie and steal and cheat."
She said, "Then you are not for me,
You are too elite."
I never went back to that café
And Trump lost the election.
The waitress came down with COVID
And took a disinfectant injection.
And no matter was he tells you,
If you mainline Clorox
You'll wind up sleeping
In a long wooden box.
They buried her on Saturday
In her bright red hat.
She wanted to make America great
But O my gosh what crap she ate,
And that, my friends, is that.

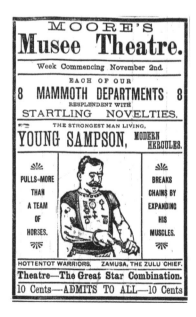

Papa Song

I'm the papa, happy to drop a bundle to make you happy.
I've paid the piper since you were in diapers, crying and feeling crappy.
I mix up your oatmeal and spoon it into your mouth.
I'm your map and your compass, I'm your north and south.
I'm the man with your bottle, I'm your faithful old pa,
I'm your horsie, your mule, your punching bag, you'd be lost without moi.
I'm the shoulder you burp on, I give you rides on my knee,
I'm your singer at two in the morning, and you'd be lost without me.

I'm the driver, the old alpha lion,
Guardian, stagehand, a shoulder to cry on.
Unplugger of toilets, the guy with the lap.
The coroner who takes mice from the trap.
Player of Uno, Pit, Checkers, and Hearts,
Teller of jokes about snot, poop, and farts.

Someday you'll throw me over for Romeo,
Though he's a fine lad, he can't be your daddy.
I am huge in your gene pool, half your biology,
I'm your best friend at three in the morning and you'd be lost without me.
And someday if you are in Dutch with the law,
At three in the morning, you're sitting in jail,
Call me, I'll come and I'll pay your bail,
I'll take you to breakfast, and I won't tell your ma.
And if you must exile to Xanadu or Scythia,
I'll be there too, right withia.

Farewell, Minnesota

Farewell, Minnesota, I'm bound for L.A.
With two hundred dollars and my screenplay.
I shaved off my hair, have a ring in my nose,
A couple of earrings, and a lot of black clothes,
A tattoo "IMAGINE" on my forehead,
And no one will guess I was born in Moorhead.
My screenplay is dark, a two-hour nightmare:
Serial killers appear everywhere,
Rampant disease, people thrown out of work,
Fascism raging, a world gone berserk.
It'll win prizes, earn a million or two,
And then I will send away, Mother, for you.
We'll live in Malibu, close to the sea.
You'll have every comfort and of course you'll have me.
We'll sit in the evening on a huge patio
And eat tuna hotdish and orange Jell-O,
And we will play Scrabble late into the night
And you'll sing me to sleep and turn out the light.
My sequel will be outrageous for sure,
But my love for you, Mother, is tender and pure.
The screen will show anarchy, catastrophe,
But at home life will be as we wish it to be.
I'll terrify millions, promote dread and fear,
And all so I can provide for you, dear.

FLY FISHING

Wading in the river,
Slipping slowly out,
Hoping to deliver
A fly to a trout.
Pole in hand, proceeding
To where the fishes lie.
Many fish are feeding,
One big fish will die.

I am free of troubles,
As the water flows,
Looking for fish bubbles,
Hit 'em on the nose.

Fishing free, unfettered,
Smoke a cigarette,
I ask you, How much better
Can a man's life get?
Up ahead my favorite spot,
A flash of silver light.
Is it—no, I guess it's not.
Thought I had a bite.

O What a Luxury

O what a luxury it be,
What pleasure O what perfect bliss,
How ordinary and yet chic
To pee, to piss, to take a leak.

To feel your bladder just go free
And open like the Mighty Miss
And all your cares go down the creek:
To pee, to piss, to take a leak.

For gentlemen of great physique
Who can hold water for one week,
For ladies who one-quarter-cup
Of tea can fill completely up,
For folks in urinalysis,
For little kids just learning this,
For Viennese or Swiss or Greek,
For everyone, how great it is
To urinate, to wee, to whiz,
To spend a penny or of course
"To see a man about a horse."

Women are quite circumspect
But men can piss with great effect,
With generous hydraulic force
Can make a stream or change its course,
Can put out fires or cigarettes.
And (sometimes) laying down our bets
Late at night outside the bars
We like to aim up at the stars.

O yes for men it's much more grand:
Women sit or squat,
We stand
And hold the fellow in our hand
And proudly watch the golden arc,
Adjust the range and make our mark
On stones and posts for rival men
To smell and not come back again.

At the Ball Game

Baseball's a slow game, no doubt.
And a fan can go strolling about
For a bratwurst with mustard
And a frozen custard,
And why not a bottle of stout?
Come back to your place,
Still no one on base,
Same score and nobody out.
You sit with your thoughts
Then notice your brat's
Incomplete and you go back for kraut.
And thoughtfully
You go off to pee
When the crowd gives out a great shout
And you wash your hands
And run back to the stands
Expecting you missed a great clout
But it's a young hound
On the field, chased around
By an usher, an ump, and a Scout.
By the 5th inning,
The other team's winning,
Five-zip, this could be a rout,
But you stay to the end
For baseball, my friend,
Is a game of faith, not of doubt.
You feel forlorn,
Buy a bag of popcorn,
And hope is reborn in the Old Scout.
Yes, hope springs eternal
And one little kernel
Can bring an end to the drought.
The bats will explode,
The bases will load,
And the Babe steps from the dugout.

FLATULENCE

Let us have another draft,
A flagon of good stout,
And leaning slightly to the left,
We'll let the gases out.
And follow this with some good wine
From the Concord grape,
And slightly to the right incline
To let the gas escape.

Flatulence O flatulence,
Why should we be aghast?
You can plug the butt and keep it shut
Till your pants inflate but you hold it in
Though nauseated and your eyeballs spin,
But the time will come at last
And what would've been a mere putt-putt
Will become a mighty blast
Like a jet plane in a dive
And the gases are ignited by a pilot light
And you come out stunned but alive,
And the story's in the *Evening Journal*:
Man's Pants Explode As He Stands At Urinal.

Henry was the King of Farts,
And he took many brides
But he dumped each one when she was stunned
By the sound of his insides.
The rumbling mutter as he stuttered and pooted,
She didn't smile. She felt defiled,
And so she was executed
Or exiled.

Exchanging gases with the atmosphere
Is a sign of life, my dear.
And why should those from the posterior
Be considered inferior?
So do not turn your back on farts
But practice them as dramatic arts,
And tighten your embouchure
To make them crisp and bright and pure,
And you can learn to talk out your ass
To make what would be a cloud of gas
Come out as, *'Twas a lover and his lass*
And lo it is a matter of fact
That through your magic powers
The songs of my digestive tract
Are sweet as summer flowers.

JACOB'S BLADDER

We're discussing Jacob's bladder, every time he pees it splatters,
And his wife is getting madder. She is really pissed.

I don't think it's bladder cancer, I told Jacob man to man, sir,
I think glasses are the answer. You can't see the pot.

He hit the floor and the shower curtain, peed on a book by Thomas
Merton, something's wrong and that's for certain. I think it's his eyes.

Urination needs precision, there's no room for indecision, Jacob's
problem's double vision. Spectacles might help.

Urine flies in all directions, he peed on the *Times* arts section.
A man who can't achieve an erection, he peed high on the wall.

Walls and floor the man's been hitting, the vandalism he's
committing, I think he should just try sitting. That will help a lot.

To stand and pee is certainly manly, David does it, Earl, and Stanley,
but Jacob's aim is quite uncannily rather off the mark.

I told Jacob, don't get hyper, but you need to pay the piper, otherwise
you'll wear a diaper, and that's when he sat down.

Now the bathroom floor is dryer, since it's out of the line of fire.
If you have a problem please inquire, and maybe I can help.

PLUMBING

In my callow youth I thought beauty and truth
And justice were what it's about,
But when facts are faced, I see life is based
On water that goes in and out.
And the plumber's the man who, when it hits the fan,
And you can't use the sink or shower stall
And the toilet will not flush and the odor makes you blush,
As the sewage rises due to turds of larger sizes,
The plumber is the man who saves us all.
People turn up their nose at the smell of his clothes,
But in crisis he's the man they call.
You confess your sins to Jesus but when your water freezes
'Cause the water heater's shut off, the shower froze your butt off,
The plumber is the man who saves us all.

Boyfriend

Susie had a lover,
His name was Sunny Jim.
She threw him in the ocean
To see if he could swim.
She threw him off a precipice
A thousand feet high
But he had a parachute
So he didn't die.
She took a bag of cyanide
And poured it in his drink.
He swallowed a gallon
And he didn't even blink.
She called him an idiot,
Told him: "Disappear."
And he just kissed her,
Said, "I'm happy to be here."
So she shot him with a pistol
But he didn't mind
Because he is imaginary:
They're the best kind.

IN THE PINES

In the pines, in the pines
We carry carbines
And we hunt the pheasant and deer.
And if you don't hunt
I'll be perfectly blunt:
Stay indoors in the fall of the year.

In the pines, in the pines
We color outside the lines
But don't be rude to your elders.
There are no writers,
Just firefighters,
Carpenters, farmers, and welders.

In the pines, in the pines,
We eat porcupines,
Rabbits, muskrats, and squirrels.
PC's for the birds,
We are men of few words,
And refer to women as "girls."

In the pines, in the pines
When the family dines
It's potatoes and smoked fish and beer.
And you may wish
That it wasn't smoked fish
But you'll eat it and be happy, my dear.

In the pines, in the pines
There are no vintage wines,
Just whiskey, vodka, and rum.
And we do not got us
Lots of Chopin sonatas
And we think that most poetry's dumb.

In the pines, in the pines
The sun seldom shines
And you work ten hours a day.
No unions, so
The pay is quite low
And spring arrives sometime in May.

In the pines in the pines
Don't expect valentines
And we are not forgiving of sins.
So never ridicule
Folks who didn't go to school
And never make fun of the Finns.

In the pines in the pines
We ignore the stop signs
And we love to go fast on the snow.
We don't use seat belts
Because it is felt
You will die when it's your time to go.

6. Love You, Darling, Indeed I Do, Cross My Heart, I Swear It's True

THE CLIMAX

of enjoyment is found by every lover of good chewing tobacco in LORILLARD'S famous

Climax Plug

Ulysses

Here by the enormous swimming pool at the Biltmore
Twenty-six young well-tanned women lie
In tiny bikinis like mermaids on the shore,
And I, bound for Ithaca, just sail on by,
Heading for you, Penelope, to tell the tale,
How that whole Trojan War gave me the willies,
The pointlessness of it, and I set sail,
Having paid off Homer and left Achilles
In his tent, and was lucky to get a favorable wind
And stopped here at the Biltmore to recompute
My course, and found twenty-six bronze-skinned
Women, their breasts displayed like fresh fruit.
    Thanks but no thanks. They only want a tan.
    You, dear, love a good story. I'm your man.

THE UNIFIED THEORY

I've been lonely as a cloud,
Drifting miserable and proud,
Lonely as a limestone butte,
Amiable but destitute,
Oh, I need you and I wait
For you and me to conjugate.

The compound that is chlorophyll
Formed as the light increases
Makes every little flower thrill
With photosynthesis.
The morning glory mingles
With the honeysuckle vine,
Come wrap your little tendrils around mine.

Nothing in nature stands alone.
Everything single thing mingles.
The tree grows out of the stone,
With other plants is intertwined:
This is what God has in mind.
And though we sit apart in church
Eventually we merge.

The Mississippi flowing south
Is never in a hurry
But it gets excited
When it marries the Missouri.
It happens down around St. Lou,
Two mighty rivers rendezvous.
I'm hoping that my dream comes true:
I'll form a mainstream with you.

Winter was horrible.
I feel alone in cold weather.
But now I hear birds warble
And we're together
In a state of undress.
Let's coalesce.

Life is just a brief rehearsal,
Then we go to the universal.
And when this life is done,
All of us will be as one,
You and I and them and we
In lovely anonymity.
Eternity we all shall reach
And find that heaven is a beach,
Then at last we understand
We are each a grain of sand
God sifts us through His hand.
Humanity in one great tide
Against our will is unified.

WAITING

A slow day in August
In my hometown.
Sun goes across the sky,
Sometimes a car goes by;
There's one right now.

A late-model Chevy
Flies past in a blur.
She drives a Chevy
But this isn't her.

She said she'd be here
Sunday or so.
Maybe by Saturday,
If she could get away.
She didn't know.

It feels sort of pitiful,
Waiting alone
Waiting for her to show.
Wishing she'd call me though
I don't have a phone.

I still believe in love,
I'm still alive.
Birds sing in angel tongues,
Small stones like diamonds
All down the drive.
Around the corner,
An old dog appears,
Sits in the summer sun
Waiting for love to come.
Wish she was here.

LOVE IN THE CORNFIELD

When the sun is out on a week before Labor Day
And we're sick of relatives, let us steal away
Out to the cornfield. I love you so.
Let's take off our clothes and go to the end of the row.

In the house they talk about their cars and their pension plans,
But you and I will have a true romance.
We'll walk to the end, just you and me.
The stalks are tall and nobody else can see.

Where the blackbirds sing and leaves are whispering,
"What do you say?" The house is far away.
What do you want? Should we yield to temptation?
The leaves are so sweet from the pollination.
You shake your head; you're afraid, I can tell.
Two Baptists kids afraid we'll go straight to hell.
So we get dressed and go back where we came from,
And I'll be thinking about you for days and weeks to come.

I'll see your naked body and my heart will throb
Every time I butter hot corn on a cob.

A Sort of Romance

It happened at my house, a raucous
Party in August.
You came with my cousin, who I thought was in
Love with you but no.
He rushed off to a show and I got a crush
On you and you knew it.
You were attractive and I was proactive
And that is the fact of the matter.
We sat on the porch by the tiki torch;
I needed you and you needed storage,
Having left your previous guy in July.
So I invited you in.
I said, "Let's do it."
You said, "Why not?"
Not how it ought to begin.
But I was available,
Stable, and capable. I could do laundry
And clean bathrooms, at least try.
I folded my clothes.
I was that kind of guy.
You were gainfully employed,
Not annoying, not in therapy,
At least not currently,
And that was good enough for me.

People thought it wouldn't last,
But these two years have sure gone fast.

You like my neatness
And my attempts at sweetness
And the part of me that is smart
Is appealing to you.

Though my French is pretentious
(You've been to France)
But my English is too.
So it's not a romance.
I don't want your heart.
Some of it might be enough,
But not the emotional stuff
And the part
About finding bliss—
But I like some of what you do.
Your taste in music is amusing,
And certain things you've said,
And the way you keep losing
Your glasses when they're parked on your head.

I have no sense of your intentions, if any.
Marriage has never been mentioned though many
Times I've wondered if I should get down on bended knee
And say, "You are my *je ne sais quoi.*"
But then I think, "Nah."
So here we are, roommates, sometimes lovers.
And every day I discover something new you've bought,
A buffet, a bureau and credenza, a birch tree in a big clay pot
You thought would look good by our bed,
Which meant you got a bigger bedstead
And a comfy cushion that's twelve feet around
For the four cats and our new greyhound.
And I think, "We may as well be in love
By virtue of the fact there is too much to dispose of."
The problem of disposal
Is the same as a marriage proposal.
We are permanently associated
By what we have accumulated.
Two loners united as owners.

LAMENT

Oh, baby, you've turned so cold to me.
What happened to our libidos?
Is this something we got from being bit by mosquitoes?
You make me feel like I'm in Minnesota.
You sit and drink your beer,
Watching football on TV for hours,
And for my birthday, dear,
You gave me tools instead of flowers.
You don't talk, you just hiccup.
Mac and cheese is your daily staple.
Instead of a car, we have a monster pickup.
You keep a jumper cable on the coffee table.

> You promised to love and honor me.
> Now I feel like I'm on the lonesome prairie
> In a severely depressed economy
> And someone is writing my obituary.
> Living in the Midwest does tend to flatten.
> How about the West Side of Manhattan?

POLARIZATION

Baby, you wrote terrible things on the wall
And you packed your clothes and drove away
With the kids to your sister's in St. Paul,
Stopping at the bank to empty our IRA.
You left the water running all afternoon,
Which I thought was rather rude,
And the front door was open and a big raccoon
Came and scarfed up all our food.
We were happy, at least I thought so,
Until we talked on the phone
About the news, and I don't know
Why but now apparently I'm all alone.
All because I made a casual aside
That I thought the Trump indictment
Was excessive—I mean, he hadn't spied
For the Russians—why the excitement?
So he took some documents by mistake.
It's poor housekeeping, give him a break.
And then you screamed when I admitted that
I voted for him once. Me, a Democrat.
"I was wrong," I said. "I know that now."
And I got home from work, and wow!
Why throw away our life, our love, our vows,
Just because I once voted to send him to the White House?
The guy's a jerk, a liar, an idiot, corrupt, rotten,
But, baby, some things are meant to be forgotten.

Saturday Night

Saturday night, just you and me,
Sit on the porch, amicably.
Ask how you are, you say, "Just fine."
I wish you would tell me what's on your mind.

What can I do to amuse you, my dear?
Where would you rather be other than here?
Do you wish you were traveling in Tuscany
With somebody other than me?

Are you wishing we'd gone to a show?
Should I have said so hours ago?
Do you feel trapped with this reclusive man?
I'm doing the best that I can.

I know I love you but I can't express
How you've brought me great happiness.
Your love makes me feel wealthy, my dear,
But I am not William Shakespeare.

I'm a Midwesterner, I don't talk much.
I wish that you'd reach over and touch
My knee and smile and whisper my name.
I wonder if you wish the same.

But you yawn and stand up instead
And announce you are heading for bed.
"Hope you have a good sleep," I said.
Is the light green or has it turned red?
Should I press the gas or is the car dead?

FAILURE

I was brilliant in my twenties,
Could've gotten a Ph.D.
I could've written a novel by now
Except you fascinate me.

You have me in your power,
And I simply acquiesce,
I'm completely absorbed by you,
And that's why my life is a mess.

On the SAT tests in school
I scored six hundred and above,
I could've been a genius by now,
But I'm a fool for your love.

And so my youthful promise
Went largely unfulfilled,
Because the moment I met you
I was completely thrilled.

We'll sit here as the honeysuckle vines
Climb up to our knees,
As termites chew the foundation
And the house falls down in a breeze.

We'll sit here in the ruins
As the years advance,
Two more tragic victims
Of a passionate romance.

DIVERSITY IN MARRIAGE

The Owl and the Pussycat went to sea,
In a beautiful catamaran.
They took a stash of negotiable cash,
Which they hid in a tunafish can.
The Owl looked up to the stars above
And sang to a blues guitar,
"O lovely Kathy, O Kathy my love,
What a very cool cat you are.
You are.
You are.
What a fabulous cat you are."

Pussy said to the Owl, "Your tender avowal
Of love is a wonderful thrill.
Let us be married before we are buried,
Let's head for Jacksonville."

Said the Owl, "Key West would make a nice nest,
Or Naples would suit my needs."
Said the elegant kitty, "A larger city
Is better for a pair of mixed breeds.
Mixed breeds.
Mixed breeds.
Is better for a pair of mixed breeds."

They sailed at once for a couple of months
To the land where the Jaguars play
And there on the beach stood a Pig who was preaching

To tourists who'd gone astray.
Astray.
Astray.
To tourists who'd gone astray.

"Dear Pig, is it possible to put down the gospel
And marry a Cat and a Bird?"
Said the pig, "For a dollar I'll put on a collar
And read you from God's Holy Word."

They dined on grits and eggs at the Ritz,
Which they ate with a silver spoon
And hand in hand they walked on the sand
Of the beach they call Neptune.
Neptune.
Neptune.
Of the beach they call Neptune.

They promised of course to share household chores
And their names they would hyphenate.
They reside in a tree and if children there be
They'll be raised in the Baptist faith.

They live on the shore where the breakers' roar,
An odd couple if you will,
But no more so than others I know
Who live in Jacksonville.
Sonville
Sonville.
Who live in Jacksonville.

GEORGE

He always wanted to sing in the opera,
Songs of passion, jealousy, rage,
While falling in love with inappropriate women,
Fighting senseless duels and dying on stage.
That's what opera is all about really,
Accepting fate, going all the way.
But he couldn't do that in Omaha, Nebraska,
Where his name was Basset but he pronounced it *Bizet*.

George was an only child in Omaha,
He joined the Scouts, he was in 4-H.
He got a blue ribbon for building a shed,
But he always dreamed of a life on stage.

He grew up Lutheran,
Polite and modest and of course repressed,
But George said, "*Non*.
There's something French in me that needs to be expressed."

He felt sort of weird
In Omaha in a black beret.
But he ate French toast
And drank his root beer with Courvoisier.

If you're shy and from the Midwest
And grow up Lutheran, it's always Lent.
He wanted music and laughter and music
But guilt was his mother's favorite instrument.
She poured him a cup of bitter black coffee,
She said, "George, it'll break our hearts if you leave."
He said, "Mama, I love you but
My *je ne sais quoi* is *joie de vivre*.

He went to Paris with Karen Larson.
He said, "It's cold here, the water tastes like copper, a
Person has to decide that there's no harm in
Living large," so he wrote her an opera
And she changed her name to Carmen.

OMG, what a passionate couple.
That rose in her teeth is fresh every day.
And if, like George Basset, you should ever visit
Paris, which you should someday,
With your amour, you might share a
Pouilly-Fuissé and do the *habanera*
Walking down the Champs-Élysées.

MOLLY MALONE

One day incognito I walked in Sausalito
And first laid eyes on Molly Malone.
She was a fishmonger and her voice was stronger
Than an earthquake siren in San Francisco.
From Marin to Palo Alto her mighty contralto
Cried, "Cockles and mussels, alive, alive-o."

I said, "Could you stifle your voice just a trifle,
Perhaps stuff a rag in your mouth, don't you know.
The right to free speech—does it mean you can screech
As you peddle your wares like a manifesto?"
Then I saw them and said, "Ma'am, those mussels look dead."
She replied, "My mussels are alive, alive-o."

Next day I saw Molly as she got off the trolley
And her voice was loud like an aerial bomb.
Along Van Ness Avenue, she hollered, "I have a new
Website, Cockles & Mussels dot com."

She gave me an oyster and I rejoiced, her
Voice was softer, and we went to a bar
And had a debacle and I ate a cockle
That had staphylococcus and went to the ER.

They pumped out my gut from gullet to butt,
And opened me up, despite my demurral,
And the surgeon, goldurn it, he took an eternity,
But he found the oyster and inside it a pearl.

I gave it to Molly and she let out a volley
Of whoopees and wahoos and yippees and cheers.
I said to her, "Yes? No?" and she took me to Fresno,
We got married and we have been happy for years.

She went on a diet and that made her quiet
And when I miss her rowdy good cheer,
I fix her clam chowder and that makes her louder
And she cries, "I love you!" so the neighbors can hear.

Winter Love

My dear, I'm sure
Our love is here to stay,
You're my thrill du jour
On a winter day.
You have nice hair, your voice is sweet,
But I love the fact you give off heat
And oxidize as we lie lengthwise,
The best heating pad I ever had.
It feels like July until the day I die
And they lay me in my grave with a little microwave
For my protection as I await the Resurrection
When we'll take angelic form and forevermore be warm.

Float Your Boat

I think the world of you
You know I wish you well
Whatever tightens your screw
Whatever rings your bell
Whatever floats your boat
Whatever greases your pan
And if poetry makes you feel carefree
Here comes the poetry man.

I know I don't know
What lights up your eyes
What makes your ketchup flow
What makes your elevator rise
But whatever it is
You know it's all right with me
And if a baritone bass can bring a smile to your face
I'll think more basically.

Some people wake up early, put their running shoes on, and take a run.
Some people go back to sleep and dream about sheep running by one by
one.

Whatever thickens your bisque
Whatever answers your prayer
Whatever downloads your disc
Whatever loads your software
Whatever pulls your cork
Whatever ripens your cheese
And if verse that rhymes can ring your chimes
Well, then I aim to please.

Some people go to parties, love the hubbub, the clamor, and the roar
Some people love to sit and listen to the moths beating gently on the old screen door.

Whatever tunes your lute
Whatever upgrades your file
Whatever peels your fruit
Whatever grouts your tile
What magnetizes your strip
Whatever fills your pies
What replaces your hip
What shapes up your thighs
Whatever chills your beer
Whatever warms your heart
And if a moment of silence puts your heart in the highlands,
Then I'll shut up.

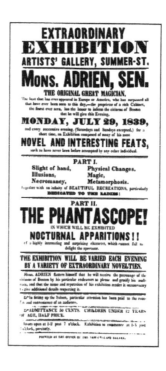

My Baby

My baby don't watch TV,
She loves the library.
She doesn't text or wear a pager,
She is an English major.
She's a true bibliophile.
She has an ear for style.
She loves the subjunctive mood,
That is her attitude:
I let her fill my senses
And conjugate my tenses.
She has style and glamour
And she uses perfect grammar,
Intuition and deduction,
I was seduced by her sentence construction.
I don't know the whys and wherefores,
But therefore I must draw the line:
Don't object if I'm subjective,
Even if it sounds possessive,
I want more of and not less of
That English major baby of mine.

SUPPER

You made crusty bread rolls filled with chunks of brie
And minced garlic drizzled with olive oil
And baked them until the brie was bubbly
And we ate them lovingly, our legs coiled
Together under the table. And salmon with dill
And lemon and whole-wheat couscous
Baked with garlic and fresh ginger, and a hill
Of green beans and carrots roasted with honey and tofu.
It was beautiful, the candles, the linen and silver,
The sun shining down on our northern street,
Me with my hand on your leg. You, my lover,
In your jeans and green T-shirt and beautiful bare feet.
   How simple life is. Supper, the smell of flowers.
   God owns tomorrow but today is ours.

Murals

Eight a.m., Monday,
I sit in this café
Looking at naked girls
Painted on old murals,
Fading away.

I grew up puritan,
Quick to condemn.
It's winter, dark and drear
Nobody's naked here
Except for them.

December, the Midwest,
A man gets depressed,
I feel mortality
Reaching for me,
Then look at that breast.

Days can be tedious
This time of year
Feels like nightfall
But I look at the wall,
Glad they are here.

I sit and work all day,
Try to write prose.
Sometimes it's okay,
Sometimes I'd like to say,
Let's take off our clothes.

Dear naked ladies,
Your painted forms
Sweet physiognomies
Withstand the winter freeze,
Keep us all warm.

Sweet naked ladies
Shine through the years.
Ladies of tenderness
Every day you undress,
Bless you, my dears.

BRISK VERSE

CORINNE

She sat in class with me,
The girl in the seat right there,
As we studied poetry
I studied her hair.
I wrote her a poem one night,
Which she never would see
For I meant nothing to her
But she was the world to me.

September was golden brown,
Cool and dry and clear.
I watched her sitting down
To read sonnets of Shakespeare.
I wrote a poem for Corinne
About what I wished would be
But I never gave it to her
Though she was the world to me.

She fell into deep despair
And put rocks in her pockets one night
And, weeping, got in her canoe
Under the full moon
And without making a sound
Tipped it over and drowned.
Now she lies in a quiet grave
And I think of what never can be.
I am nothing to her
She remains the world to me.

I think of that moonlit night.
Imagine I'm out for a walk
And see the flickering light
As she moves to the end of the dock.
I want to speak but I can't,
It all goes by in a flash,
The canoe rocks aslant,
And I hear the splash.
It happens over and over.
She climbs into the canoe.
I think I'm going to save her
But I never do.

BREAKFAST

Arising Monday morning
An hour before dawn,
Picked up the morning paper,
Put the coffee on.
The news is beyond comprehension,
Suffering everywhere.
To read it would be deadening
So I set it on the chair.
I toast a sesame bagel,
Fresh coffee in the air,
And then the lovely music
Of your feet upon the stair.
In an old blue bathrobe,
Sunlight in your hair.

And suddenly it's meaningful
To be standing here.
And when I take you in my arms
Everything is clear.
Your voice and eyes and skin,
You standing next to me,
This is where my world begins
In simple clarity.
Here is half a bagel
Toasted with cream cheese.
Sitting at this table,
We two touching knees.

From here we welcome Monday
And we go pursue
The various and sundry
That we're put here to do.
You play music, go for walks,
Embrace society,
I sit and stare at a screen in a box
At prose and poetry.
Right here is our Eden
And the light divine
In this quiet meeting,
Your life touching mine.

My Violist and Me

I'll never forget the night we met,
She was playing Bizet at the Café Tête-à-Tête,
The only viola in the famous St. Paul string quartet.

Her bowing was strong, the fingering precise,
Then they swung into Stravinsky's partita "Paradise,"
Which took my heart, a great big slice.

Violins sound scratchy and whiny,
But her viola was mellow, sunshiny,
Big and bold, not fragile and tiny.

They swung into the Rolling Stones' "Jumpin' Jack Flash,"
The dancers jumped up and made a mash,
And they passed a hat to collect the cash.

From "Jumpin' Jack" they jumped into Brahms
As a nod to the dads and moms
And then Little Richard and she switched to tom-toms,
Played "Long Tall Sally" and brought down the house,
People went crazy, then they took their bows
And slipped into something by Richard Strauss.

I bought her a drink during intermission.
She wasn't stuck up like a classical musician.
Her eyes met mine, I could feel ignition.
"Right now you're sitting in a string quartet,"
I said, "but you ain't seen nothing yet.
You and me, we are major creators."
And she formed a band, The Violators.

She was the greatest rock 'n' roll viola,
She became a brand like Coca-Cola.
She jumped around like Punchinello,
The viola was bright orange and yellow,
She made it wail, she made it bellow,
At the finale she burned a cello.
Giant football stadia we'd play.
New York to L.A. and around the U.K.
Viola, drums, guitar, synthesizer.
I drove bus, was strategic advisor.

We were red-hot for seventeen months.
Then she said, "I've done it once,
And once is enough. I've rocked, let's roll."
So we did the last show at the Hollywood Bowl.
Came home to Connecticut, bought us a manse
Where she can hike and tend her plants,
Work the crossword to sharpen her wits,
While I sit and write the hits.
I wrote Lizzo, most of Taylor Swift,
Mariah Carey, it's just my gift.
And on a shelf, her three violas,
They're planters now, full of gladiolas,
Blossoming beautifully, silently,
Just like her and Baby and me.

MAY

I am fond of May,
When March has completely passed away,
A month whose definition
Is "to give permission,"
When a luxurious sun
Shines on everyone
And robins sing cheerily and sincerely.
Soft ice cream dipped in butterscotch,
Which you watch
Being sold for a buck at the ice cream truck.
And though you feel derelict,
Being on a strict
No-butterscotch diet,
You try it.
People working the crossword in the sun,
And twenty-one
Down
Is a noun
That's a verb
Meaning "jump the curb
When you hear bells ding":
Reveling? Rollicking? Gamboling? Wassailing?

SPRING

The smell of yellow forsythia
Stays with you
And the narcissus
Is auspicious,
The cherry blossom awesome,
As one thrills
To daffodils
And focuses
On crocuses
And even the dandelion
Can be satisfyin'.

People don the clothing of romance,
Lilac loungewear and paisley pants,
Thinking outside the box,
Heliotrope tops and strawberry socks,
A woman passes
Wearing purple sunglasses
And shiny shorts with terrific tights
Embroidered with tiny flashing lights
And a seafoam green tank top with embroidered flowers
Exercising mysterious tank top powers
That cause even Methodist men
To turn sharply to look again
And sprain their necks
Contemplating uncomplex
Subjects and convex objects
And the activity
Of creativity,
In other words, sex.

DAUGHTER

I found my daughter a safe haven
Where the hurricane won't blow a wave in.
Safe from wolves and the danger
Of the smooth-talking stranger
And no bears come in the yards,
Where good neighbors are the guards.
I am old and when I die
A circle will solidify
Around my girl—family, friends,
Along with monthly dividends
From the assets that I saved
Back when I was well-behaved.
The mansion that I didn't buy,
The July we didn't fly to Lanai
But visited Wichita instead,
Will make an umbrella over her head.
God will provide and also the neighbors
But some is due to your father's labors.
And after I've gone to the hereafter
I hope she remembers all the laughter.

Summer Night

Northern town on a summer night,
Gardenias pink and white,
Shotgun houses on a quiet street
And the air is sweet.

Birches and a maple tree.
In their shade sit you and me,
Our two hands intertwine
Like the honeysuckle vine.

Bullfrogs on the river shore,
Mockingbird in the sycamore,
Singing songs to their mates
And a grasshopper ruminates.

The far-off whistle of a southbound train,
You lean in close and say my name.
God forbid, our love gets old,
Hands go free and hearts grow cold.

Day by day is how we live;
Do our best and the rest forgive.
Crickets murmur in the grass,
The train goes through and the hours pass.

Hand in hand and head to head,
Much we know need not be said.
Here and now is completely clear.
Today is the best day of the year.

Stick with Me

I would climb mountains, swim the seas,
I would eat live bumblebees,
I could be witty and effervescent
If women were present.

Somehow women make me braver.
If one fell overboard, I'd save her,
Run barefoot across burning decks,
Anything for the gentle sex.

Michelangelo had strong feeling
For Sistine so he painted her ceiling.
Bach was passionate, which would explain a
Family of kids with Anna Magdalena.

Shakespeare's sonnets were a shady
Pathway to his dear dark lady.
Baryshnikov found dance an occasion
Not only for art but fornication.

If it weren't for women, we men would squat
Around the fire and grunt a lot,
Never bathe or change the sheets,
Throw our garbage in the street.

If you'd been raised by your pop,
He might've raised you or let you drop.
Heaven saved you from the drama
Of growing up without a mama,
The loneliness, the sheer despair,
Not knowing how to comb your hair,
What food to eat, which shirt to wear.
She taught you manners, gave you style,
Showed how life can be worthwhile,
And how to behave and what to say
When a fair young woman comes your way.

7. GEOGRAPHY

MINNESOTA

She lived in San Francisco
In the cool Pacific mists
Where she danced all night to disco
With the other hedonists.
A life of ease and sushi
And yet she felt depressed.
And one afternoon at two she
Took a plane to the Midwest.

She went to Minnesota
To discover what life means,
A place where people go ta
Get away from limousines,
A state where people know to
Wear long johns beneath their jeans.

Oh, people come from Wall Street
To find out how they feel,
The street where you see the false treat-
Ed as if it were real.
Although wildly successful
And wearing many hats,
They found it rather stressful
Trying to race with younger rats.
Presbyterians, whom John Knox taught
That life is a stone wall,
Come to learn the foxtrot
In the city of St. Paul.

A Boston Unitarian
Found Minnesota: in it he
Came to love the prairie and
Believed in the Trinity.

Rich folks leave their chauffeurs
And atone for their sins
By rooting for the Gophers,
The Vikings and the Twins.
If you're feeling frustration
And it's time to go straight,
Minnesota's your destination:
It is the North Star state.

GEOLOGY

Manhattan gneiss, Manhattan schist
Enable New York to exist.
G-n-e-i-s-s,
Metamorphic, igneous.
S-c-h-i-s-t
Lying under you and me,
Eighteen feet under Times Square
Where towers rise into the air.

Tall buildings need a base, a dock,
Otherwise they're apt to list.
No matter how you slice or dice.
You better build on a hill of schist.

Geology, geology,
Underlies all you see.
Not so good for the farming sector,
But it's great for architecture.

Otherwise it'd be a swamp,
Much more mushrooms, much less pomp.
All the towers on this block
Are anchored on solid rock.

In the Ice Age, glaciers slid
Across the land like giant blades,
Moving mountains. Yes, they did,
And they made the Palisades.

And if there is a flood again
Sent by God as a sign to men,
The spot where we will build the ark
Will be on a hill in Central Park,
Near the Museum of Natural Hist
On a mountain of Manhattan schist.
And if we go to paradise,
That hill of schist will sure be gneiss.

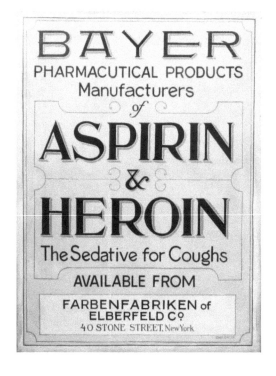

KANSAS

Kansas is flat with occasional rises
And it's a long way between surprises.
Not many towers or billboards or trees
And all the motels have vacancies.
Flat land and straight barbed wire,
Lots of equality: not much is higher.
So expectations are low, as such.
You can Fast-Forward and not find much.
It's easily forgotten and quickly crossed,
Any tourist is probably lost.
The weather is either cold or hot.
It's not what you wanted, it's what you got.
You can die of sunstroke or freeze your shorts.
Thank goodness for football and price supports,
Republican politics, low taxes,
The Baptist church, and cable access.
Once you come, if you stay
You're building character every day.
Wake up, drink coffee, go out and thresh.
And watch where you step, it may be fresh.

Kansas is God's way of suggesting
Life doesn't need to be interesting.
He was busy elsewhere fighting sin;
When he made Kansas, he phoned it in.
The land is flat, the wind is blowing,
The state is halfway to where you're going.
But if we seem sleepy or in a coma
You know, we're looked up to by Oklahoma.

AMAZON

I'm growing tired of the Northern Hemisphere,
Life is so dreary this time of year.
In all my dreams I am roaming once more
With my pals on the shores of Brazil and Ecuador.
Miss those corn tortillas
And the sweet guitars,
The buenos días of señoritas
In tequila bars.
Why am I in Minnesota
Instead of in Peru?
I am so alone, I miss *amor, mi corazón.*
Miss the Amazon and you.

They have sumptuous summers down there in January.
They're very carefree while we're freezing on the prairie.
So put your silk pajamas on,
Mama, you look so fine.
Let's go to the Amazon,
Not the one that sells online
And is happy to deliver—
No, I mean the mighty river,
Where the richest and the poorest,
The tourist or the purist,
The scholar and folklorist,
Can explore the rain forest
And snakes and cockatoos
And crocodiles can amuse,
Let's you and me entwine
Swinging from a jungle vine.
I'm dreaming, love, it's true,
Dreaming of the Amazon and you.

POEM FOR JENNY

I have a Midwestern affliction,
A disposition to brood
And put myself in a sad mood
A few feet away from my wife,
Staring into the air
As if she isn't there
And think about the vagaries of life.

But I walk around New York (boom boom)
Amid the jazz and razzmatazz,
The drummers whapping on the plastic pails,
The shaking of the subway on the rails,
The anti-fur protest,
The guy with a snake wound around his chest,
The street corner preacher and the *quack quack* man
Arguing with a garbage can,
    And when all is said,
      It's a good way to go to get out of your head.

Here in the bustle and the roar,
You can't feel sorrowful any more.
You watch the St. Patrick's Day parade
Undismayed, all of your complaints and gripes
Are blown away by cops in skirts playing bagpipes.
If you want gloom, go to Grant's Tomb
Or Woodlawn Cemetery up in the Bronx,
Manhattan is for the clamor of jackhammer, sirens, honks.
Thoreau hated Manhattan.
He sat in Concord consulting with the Lord
In his little cabin on Walden Pond

With a table for one and a straight-back chair,
Staring into the Eternal Beyond.
I'd rather look at that six-story blonde
On the billboard for American Air,
A flight attendant who makes me feel transcendent.

I made mistakes, I lost some bets,
I did what I did and have no regrets.
No therapy for me, no weepy memoir.
The place that I would like to be
Is right here where we are
In New York—
A great old walking town.
Uptown's up and downtown's down,
East is east and west is west.
Take the local or the express
From Harlem down to the Trinity steeple.
New York's where you see all the people
And it's where I found you, 1992.
I could've searched the world wide
But here you were on the Upper West Side.
They could put up a plaque on the spot.
Three years later we tied the knot
In an Episcopal chapel in the Big Apple,
Said, "I do" and so did you.
You, a girl from my hometown,
Came out east to knock 'em dead,
Find fortune and renown
And you got me instead.
What an adventure it has been.
What say, we do it again?

L.A.

There are few orange groves in Orange County.
Manhattan Beach is not New York, no way.
There isn't much adventure in Ventura
But you can sit and bake in Bakersfield all day.
Oakland? You've got to be joking.
Sunnyvale is far from radiant.
Berkeley? What have you been smoking?
Ontario is Canadian.
There's nothing that surprising in Eureka
And San Jose—what can I say?
There's not much holy in Sacramento
But it's sandy in San Diego Bay.

People can be salty in Salinas.
Fremont's a long way from free.
I'm happy to pass Pasadena.
Long Beach is too long for me.

Santa Monica has no sleigh and reindeer.
St. Francis would be shocked by his Bay.
And nobody's that modest in Modesto
But I must say I love L.A.
I've felt wayward in Hayward.
I've had the blues in Santa Cruz.
Been in ill huma in Petaluma.
But I must say, I love L.A.
C. I. N. … D.E.R. … E.L.
L.A.

MINNEAPOLIS

To the Mississippi River that supplied the power
To cut lumber and make Pillsbury's Gold Medal Flour,
The old man comes
Who remembers these warehouses that became condominiums
Where joggers with waistbelts with waterbottles stretch for their run
And people of diverse ethnicities wait for public transportation.
I worry about my city, being 81,
Even in the June sunshine
Reflecting off the glass towers of the skyline—
Rising from the prairie in modest splendor,
I feel an old man's tender concern about my hometown under the blue sky
To which I have bid goodbye.
My mother grew up on Longfellow & 38th
And was brought up in the Christian faith.
And her family lies in a modest section
Of Lakewood Cemetery awaiting resurrection,
Looking out on Lake Harriet and Lake Bde Maka Ska
Like a pastoral painting by Delacroix
Under a sky with streaks of white fleece
Like a Matisse masterpiece.
A man leaves home to back away from back then
And be young and unknown again
And draw a curtain on the dead
And be interested in what lies ahead.
But now it all comes back,
The yellow streetcar stops on the track,

Mother takes my hand and we climb aboard,

The conductor yanks on the cord,

The bell clangs and we rumble toward

Downtown and Dayton's Department Store,

Which isn't there anymore,

But enough about that. Memory, shut up.

Take my hand, Buttercup,

And let's head east.

God grant peace to the deceased.

Soon enough each one of dies.

Let's go watch the sun rise.

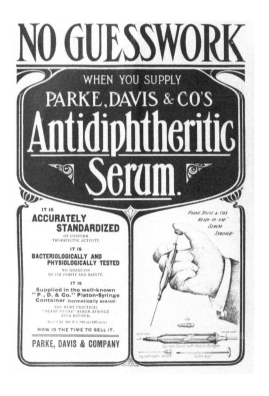

St. Paul Blues

She had bright red hair and I tried not to stare
At her gown, which was low and strapless.
I wanted to dance but I didn't stand a chance
For she was from Minneapolis.
And her icy glare as she stared at me there
Made me feel two feet tall.
She could see that I'm strictly small-time,
She could see that I'm from St. Paul.

You can strut your stuff and be dressed to kill
But they can see you're from Nowheresville,
You're someone they look right through,
They are so not into you.
They're big league, you're Class D ball.
You can get a facelift, fix your chin recess,
Have a hair transplant on your chest,
Buy a Rolex and a Cadillac,
Armani clothes, everything black,
Fake an accent, it's a perfect disguise,
You go to Minneapolis, they just roll their eyes.

St. Paul is the capital, we have the archdiocese,
But Minneapolis has its biases,
And we're just a big small town.
They're Ray Charles, we are Charlie Brown.
I got mint deodorant, a fresh new smell,
New mouthwash, sprayed on Chanel,
Put lifts in my shoes to make me tall,
But still they could tell I'm from St. Paul.

HYMN TO THE FARM

Morning light soft and bright, Wobegon reveals
Early frost, all across farm and woods and fields.
Coffee done, I'll have some, step outside alone,
Look around, set me down, on a slab of stone.
By the barn, cattle turn, murmur in the pen.
Soft and pure, cow manure:
I am home again.

Precious Lord, by your word
Simple gifts are blest.
Let the promise of salvation
Come by daily observation
In this farmyard, Lord, be with us.

My old dog takes his walk, sniffing every tree.
Every smell seems to tell his biography.
Chickens dash 'cross the grass.
Cats patrol the yard;
Seven geese marching east, form an honor guard.
Then the small trumpet call, ringing to the skies
Three loud barks, arf, arf, arf.
Wake up and arise, be in paradise.

The Bells of Minnesota

We are humble but proud
Say the bells of St. Cloud.

In the dark, light a candle
Say the bells of St. Wendel.

The Lord only knows
Say the bells of Melrose.

This world God inhabits
Say the bells of Sauk Rapids.

Every bird the Lord knows of
Say the bells of St. Joseph.

This is not a resort
Say the bells of Freeport.

Dig the ground, plant a garden
Say the bells of St. Martin.

Make the rows even
Say the bells of St. Stephen.

Plant a row, pound a stake
Say the bells of Clear Lake.

Sow the seed even-handedly
Say the bells of St. Anthony.

Paint your house, mow your lawn
Say the bells of Avon.

Then sit on your porch
Say the bells of St. George.

All is well, all is well
Say the bells of Sartell.

8. ALPHABETICAL

A boy from Anoka named Gary
Was lonesome out on the prairie
Among Christian folks
Who never told jokes
Or swore, even when necessary.
I tried to write limericks in school
In hope it would make me popular.
I tried and I tried
And some were not bad,
But something seemed to be missing.

The Beatles said all that you need
Is love, which is lovely indeed,
And I don't take issue
And yet toilet tissue
Is useful too, one must concede.

C

A fine old man from the City
Formed a campaign committee
But gave up the race
When he saw that his face
Looked just like his butt, what a pity.

A third-grade teacher named Dede
Came home to her squeeze and said, "Sweetie,
I'm worn out and wobbly
So pour me a Chablis
And don't be emotionally needy."

E

Here's to my friend Evelyn
With whom I was tempted to sin
And be wild and obscene
When we were eighteen
And now it's too late to begin.

Why didn't we neck in the car
Or swim naked off the sandbar?
We had many chances
At parties and dances
And yet remained chaste. How bizarre.

Time is not something to save
For later. Buck up and be brave.
O let it be known,
Children, do not postpone
Adventure. Rise up. Misbehave.

F

I do not belong in First Class.
In high school, I barely could pass.
Helen Hunt taught Latin
And the chair that I sat in
Was not in front, you bet your ass.

G

George was from St. Paul and not
Fond of cold winters and got
Away one day
To Santa Fe,
Had a heatstroke and died on the spot.
The widow decamped for Key West
And lay in the sunshine undressed
And was broiled and fried,
Got cancer and died,
Was cremated, then laid to rest.
Her oldest boy tried a high-rise
In Miami where to his surprise
A white albatross
High on hot sauce
Dove down and pecked out his eyes.
His sister in Key Biscayne
Recovered from sorrow and pain
Through gentle massage,
Which released a barrage

Of blood clots into her brain.
Her husband, John, cried, "Aha!"
And bought a place in Panama
Where a poisonous snake
Jumped out of a cake
And bit him and also his ma.
His nephew went to Cancún
And joined a Moonie commune
And cashed in his chips
When a lunar eclipse
Made him swoon and choke on a prune.
His brother tried to persist, he
Headed for Corpus Christi
But the weather was misty,
The highway was twisty
And covered with slime,
And it doesn't rhyme
But he slammed into a bridge abutment.
One daughter, observing this all,
Moved back to live in St. Paul.
She's now eighty-three,
Lives happily
Near me and goes nowhere at all.
The quest for comfort and ease
Led to severe tragedies.
They crashed and burned
And nobody learned:
Man should not curse it, he
Thrives on adversity.
God send us cold winters, please.

This limerick's in honor of Him
Who asked to be left anonym,
Turning three score and ten
On earth among men
And not among bright seraphim.
A loyal prairie progressive
Suspicious of pomp and excessive
Wealth and such
And making too much
Out of what there ought to be less of.
His entire life has been graced
By common sense and good taste
And two rules in mind:
Always be kind
And avoid (if possible) waste.

I

I have to make an admission:
I never hear *Morning Edition*
Except during Lent
At the convent
Where it's meant as an act of contrition.

J

There was an old lady named Jude
Who, imagining her solitude,
In warm weather chose
To take off her clothes
And walk around town in the nude
And old men and rubes
Would stare at her boobs
And think thoughts licentious and lewd.
She was eighty, Miss Judy,
And not a great beauty
But O how she lightened the mood.

K

A lady named Katherine Lee Bates
Sang "America the Beautiful" on skates
As she sailed round the rink
And according to her shrink
That was why no one asked her on dates.

L

Luther College stands in Decorah,
Far from Sodom, far from Gomorrah.
Each student is lent
A New Testament,
Which they read by the light from their aura.

M

Minneapolis is great. Have you seen it?
The streets go from Aldrich to Zenith.
It's the birthplace of Prince,
Than whom no one since
Has been any hipper, I mean it.
The city is good for the sickly.
The streets are numerical, strictly,
And alphabetical
All so that medical
Teams can get to you quickly.

N

Nixon was a desperate crook
At whom history will throw the book
Just for the war
He was on the hook for
Prolonging and the lives that it took.
A classic schlump and a schnook,
He should've been hung on a hook
And shown no mercy
But he moved to New Jersey,
Forsaken (or is it forsook?).

O

Old times I cannot forget
When the stories were bawdy, you bet,
And we sat smoking smokes
And told dirty jokes
Until everyone's trousers were wet.

P

There was a poet named Perry,
Took pills to feel extraordinary,
Did opium, speed,
Smoked bundles of weed,
Drank absinthe, cognac, and sherry.
The effect was astonishing. Very.
He wrote so much it was scary.
And then by and by
He asked himself, "Why
Am I lying in this mortuary?"
His friends assembled to carry
The urn to the town cemetery,
A gust of wind blew,
And the ashes all flew,
Leaving nothing of Perry to bury.
His memory was kept
By the sexton who swept
Up the dust. God heal
Our souls. He is real
And now Perry's imaginary.

Q

Quentin did not go for hip,
A gypsy off on a trip.
He put on a suit
And felt absolute-
Ly fine with a brown leather grip.
Style is b.s. Just live
And muster the gifts you can give.
Some very profound
Radicals walk around
Looking prim and conservative.

R

Rhonda, a Baptist of Aspen
Fell down groanin' and gaspin'.
She thought she'd been bit
By a snake on her tit
But it was her Sunday school class pin.
That night Rhonda headed for Reno
And stayed up late playing keno
On the strength of some pills
And the sight of large bills
And a handsome young dealer named Gino.
She was taken with him,
His fingers so slim,
He was graceful and suave and Latino,
And she felt not so bad
As she lost all she had,
Including her cherry (maraschino).

S

There was an attractive stockbroker
Who beat everybody at poker.
Her blouse was revealing
And also concealing
The ace of hearts and the joker.

T

We cruise on a ship 'cross the sea
And experience mortality
On the Atlantic shelf
Where in 1912,
Anguished and frantic,
The good ship Titanic
Slipped under the wave
To its watery grave.
I hold my breath
And think about death
And you put your arm around me.

U

There was an old Unitarian,
A ferocious Christmas contrarian.
"God was not made flesh,"
He said, so his crèche
Was a room with just Joseph and Mary in.

V

A lady who lived in Vancouver
Drank two quarts of varnish remover
And did not get ill
And vomit, but still,
It didn't do much to improve her.

W

We live by humor and grace,
Good manners, books, an embrace,
Good water, good light,
A pencil to write,
And a bright orange stub to erase.

X

X marks the Upper West Side
Where a man lived, so satisfied,
Till at age fifty-five
He went for a drive
To Vermont, caught pneumonia, and died.

Y

Youth is a fabulous pill—
Instilling the thrill of free will
And crazed liberty—
And, fortunately,
A prescription one cannot refill.

Z

Zelda, a liberal of D.C.
By day was tasteful and PC.
And then after ten
She went out with men
Who were rednecks, vulgar, and greasy.
"When it comes to the masculine specie,"
She said, "believe me, I'm easy,
But liberal guys
Tend to theologize,
And I am not St. Clare of Assisi."

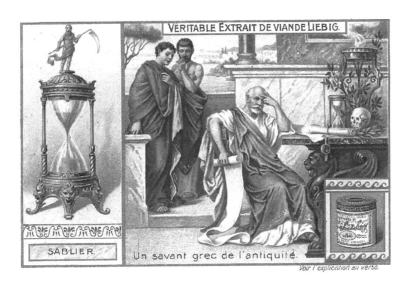

VÉRITABLE EXTRAIT DE VIANDE LIEBIG.

SABLIER.

Un savant grec de l'antiquité.

Voir l'explication au verso.

9. GREAT WRITERS

Miss Austen, the valiant Jane,
Abstained from gin and cocaine
And consorting with men,
But now and again
She was thrilled to take walks in the rain.

The tortured poet John Berryman
Was a strange, alcoholic, and scary man.
He might've been stronger
And lived a lot longer
Had he been a truck driver or dairyman.

Teenagers love E.E. Cummings
For his romantic hummings and strummings
And his embrace
Of The All-Lower Case
And he didn't write long but short, Cummings.

Dear Emily D. of Amherst
Seldom shouted or cursed
Except when the birds
Dropped little white turds,
She said, "Poop," but that was the worst.

We read T.S. Eliot in school,
And *The Waste Land* struck us as cruel,
So we dropped out of class,
Got a job pumping gas
And made friends with girls, which was cool.

A true Yankee was Robert Frost
Who seldom went out and got sauced,
Didn't write elegies
To disgrace and disease
And feeling hopelessly lost.

An Ohio dentist, Zane Grey,
Wrote Westerns, yippee-i-ay.
Today he's not read,
We have TV instead,
But he's dead so I'm sure it's okay.

Hemingway wound up his journey
In a long depressing downturn—he
Picked up a gun
As his father had done,
And they wrapped Ernie up on a gurney.

The letter I, naturally,
Is meant to represent me.
The writer, myself,
My books on your shelf,
My voice speaking symbolically.

Henry James preferred the obscure,
The elaborate scenic detour—
You say, "Coffee or tea?"
He replies lengthily—
Yes or no? You cannot be sure.

Kafka was lonely in Prague
And lived in a neurotic fog,
Groaning and keening
And longing for meaning—
He should've just gotten a dog.

A troubled man, Robert Lowell,
Was bipolar deep in his soul,
And despite his great gifts,
He worked double shifts
Deep in the mine digging coal.

Herman Melville's book *Moby-Dick*
Is not only dense, it is thick.
And the trip *to* the ship
Is a slow drip-drip-drip,
So I think I'll just wait for the flick.

A formalist Nemerov (Howard)
Believed that a poem is powered
By attention to time,
Space, rhythm, and rhyme,
That free verse is the work of a coward.

The poet of life Mary Oliver
Every day harked to the call of her
Flowers and birds
And put into words
The entirety, everything, all of her.

Poor dear Sylvia Plath
Was torn up by sorrow and wrath.
The day that she dove
Headfirst in the stove,
She should have just run a hot bath.

Question: are limericks art,
Possessing a soul and a heart,
Or simply the smile
Of innocent guile
After a small pungent fart?

Theodore Roethke (or Ted)
Grew up in a greenhouse, he said.
For all of his faults,
He wrote "My Papa's Waltz,"
Which truly deserves to be read.

Edna St. Vincent Millay
Was a love goddess back in the day,
Green eyes and red hair
And bohemian flair.
She tangled with men
And girls now and then,
Which gave her plenty to say.
After many affairs,
She slipped on the stairs,
And died, which is not the worst way.

The great transcendental Thoreau
Went to live in the woods long ago
And wrote lovely prose
While his mom washed his clothes
And fixed him hot lunches to go.

The prodigious productive Updike
Wrote prose like riding a bike,
Fiction, reviews,
Verse to amuse,
Throwing strike after strike after strike.

A poet named Wordsworth, old Bill
Liked to climb to the top of a hill
And sit spellbound for hours
Looking at flowers
This was years before movies, but still.

The poet X.J. (Joe) Kennedy,
In Ireland, would be in the Senate. He
Is up there with Yeats,
But here in the States,
A poet is a minor amenity.

Y, my dear reader, is You,
Without whom what writers do
Has little meaning
Like a tree that is leaning
And falls in the woods out of view.

And Z is for zest and pizzazz,
Which all great literature has,
The song and the beat
Of feet in the street,
The juice and the joy and the jazz.

The National Anthem

As it might have been written had another poet than F.S. Key been present in Baltimore harbor in 1814.

1. WALT WHITMAN

Here on the shore of Baltimore observing the barrage of rockets and bombs from the man-o'-war,
The gunnery mates stripp'd to the waist and glistening with sweat,
Shouting each to the other and working together in close drill,
Ramming the powder charge and then the enormous projectile,
Each of them a man like myself and possessed of secret longings,
Each of them comely and well-appointed,
Especially the tall one on the left with black curls and taut abdominal muscles,
Who looks so long and lovingly at me, a stranger in big boots,
And I return his gaze—O afficionado, come, take my hand—
Leave your cannonading and we shall travel the open road
Where there are no banners except of affection and the love of dear comrades.

2. EMILY DICKINSON

The Banner ---- that we watched in Air
So Proudly as it Gleamed
Was Proven by the Rocket Glare
Or so to us it Seemed ----

And so we waited for the Dawn
To see if it still flew
Or if ---- in Tatters ---- it is Gone ----
As happened once ---- with You.

I woke up ---- at the Matin Bell ----
A vast and empty Bed ----
The Pillow bore --- the slightest smell
Of Oil ---- from your Head.

A fleeting Phantasy ---- perhaps ----
The Ghost of ---- Not To Be ----
And Postmen ---- in their Crimson Caps ----
Aim their Artillery.

3. ROBERT FROST

Whose flag this is I think I know
His house is being bombed now though
He will not see that I have come
To watch the twilight's ebbing glow.

My little horse must think it dumb,
The cannons' pandemonium,
The rockets bursting in the air,
The sound of bugle, fife, and drum.

He turns and shakes his derriere
To show me that he doesn't care
Who takes this battle flag or why,
When in the redness of the glare

I see the banner flying high
Through the tumult in the sky
And, knowing all is now okay,
We walk away, my horse and I.

The flag is lovely, hip hooray,
But I have things to do today,
Some here and others far away,
Before I stop to hit the hay.

4. T.S. ELIOT

—Auprès de ma blonde, qu'il fait bon dormir.

Alas, I grow old and may not see
The dawn shantih shantih
But I shall stay up as late as I can,
Hoping it will rain.

Do I dare to sing a song?
What if I forget the words
And the high notes are beyond my reach
And I should screech
And the mermaids look at me and think,
Twit twit twit twit twit?
O it is the cruellest song.

In the dark the rockets come and go.
Or maybe bombs, I do not know.
O say, can you see?
I can't.
I hope they do not fall on me.

5. MARIANNE MOORE

Saliently and with salutary heraldic
Vigor—verging on "insouciance"—
Flutters the gallant chevron
Claret & turquoise & *blanc de blanc*—of stellar striation.
"It's a grand old flag," my father said once,
Waving it with cursive undulations.
Now hid amidst the taupe and topaz of smoke; nocturnally
Tenacious, "gallant under fire,"
It flaunts a high standard;
Illuminated by aggression expressed thus thunderously—
O felicitous ballistics!

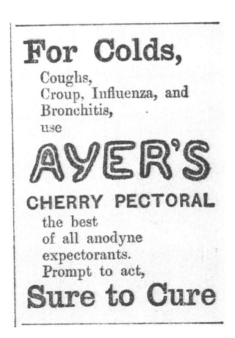

6. WILLIAM CARLOS WILLIAMS

This is just to say
I have taken
The flag
That was
flying

And which
You probably expected
To see
This morning

Forgive me
It was beautiful
So free
And so brave

7. ROBERT BLY

"We know we are here because it is so dark." —Rumi

It is dark in Minnesota,
And the flag we saw at twilight
Flutters like my grandmother looking for her spectacles
Or like an owl floating over the corn stubble looking for dinner.

She arises at dawn and everything is as it was.
What we see is what we have seen before,
Nothing has changed. The grass is spangled with drops of dew
Like the Milky Way
And also with the droppings of pigeons.
Let us be brave and go home.

8. BILLY COLLINS

On the ship, I sit and wait for the dawn
In the midst of the bombs and rockets and so forth,
A prisoner of these British marines who might shoot me,
You never know in a situation like this.

Like so many great moments in history,
You come upon it without meaning to.
You're a lawyer who goes to negotiate for the release of a prisoner
And voilà, you become one yourself.

There is this incredibly perilous fight going on
And I suppose a person should be thinking about freedom
Or bravery but I must admit
I would give anything for a cup of coffee right now.
I wonder what's going to happen to that flag.

Somebody could write a poem about this,
Something to mark this whole thing that's going on,
But if they did, probably they shouldn't include
The part about wanting a cup of coffee.

Reader

Holly Golightly takes a taxi down to Tiffany's
As Holden Caulfield walks west in a hurry.
She is calmed by the sight of diamond jewelry
And he by the solidity of the Museum of Natural History.

And A.J. Liebling walks along 43rd toward Times Square,
One o'clock in the morning and all the tourists are gone.
He stops at his watering hole and if there are no friends there
He makes some new ones. "A wonderful, grand old Babylon."

Christmas lights in the windows of brownstones,
O. Henry's story lingering there.
Jim pawned his watch to buy Della combs,
To buy him the watch chain, she sold her hair.

Jay Gatsby walks to the end of his great yard,
Leaving the party, the dancers going round and round,
And looks at the green light out there in the dark,
A distant dock across Long Island Sound.

Men in fresh suits and gray felt hats
Come striding out of Grand Central Station,
Salesmen, CEOs, Renaissance aristocrats,
Direct from John Cheever's rich imagination.

Edna St. Vincent Millay in her summer dress
Stands at the window in love with somebody.
E.B. White said: New York bestows the gift of loneliness. No one
should come to live here unless willing to be lucky.

And so in New York, I feel at ease
In crowds of strangers hereamong,
From the East 20s to the West 90s,
Walking through books I read when I was young.

An Average Poem

I got a so-called college education
For which I paid tuition,
But frankly the train never left the station.
There was no key in the ignition,
They taught us (they thought) to think clearly,
The art of living on a rational basis,
And we students settled for shininess merely,
Which, admit it, is good enough in most cases.

Most of the time, my mind is on holiday,
Not focused on quality.
I'm okay with hip-hop, Pop Art, sliders, the romance novel.
You go to a movie that's rather awful
And afterward climb into the Chev and you
Realize why it brought in so much revenue.
No matter what you were taught,
More people are average than not.
It's lonely at the top but it'll
Be very comfortable in the middle.

This poem, for example: it's not terrible.
No, it doesn't soar, doesn't even climb.
It's not the Sermon on the Mount or the parable
Of the prodigal son.
But it's worth a minute of your time,
And then it's done.

Genius is so underhanded
And people who admire it are proud
To be among the few who understand it;
Me, I like to be in a crowd.
Some people grapple with the herculean
And strive for the golden apple,
But that's not the crowd I wish to be in;
I prefer the rabble.
I have a feeling
That if asked to do the Sistine Chapel ceiling,
You would and I would
Have used quarter-inch plywood.
And instead of a Michelangelo,
It would be more like a bungalow.

A bungalow is good enough.
God is not in need of grandeur,
Grandeur he already has plenty of,
He wants your praise and your
Obedience and your hearts.
Jesus did not participate in the arts
While on earth, didn't do ballet,
Didn't even crochet,
He never wished
To write poetry. He fished.

So I'm not hoping for the Nobel Prize.
It's too big for my desk.
I don't want to be statuesque.
I'm just one of the guys
In the literature occupation
Worthy of honorable mention.
Thanks for your attention.

"The fragrance of pipe tobacco makes
me wish I were a man".....*Bbe Daniels*

10. LAST WORDS

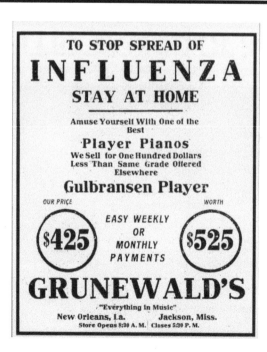

Thong Song

I am looking at your butt crack,
A.k.a. the gluteal cleft.
Either way, it's at the bottom of your back
Between the one on the right and the one on the left.

On this matter, my mind is shut:
Don't walk around showing off your butt.
Don't walk around half-naked at least
Until I am safely deceased.

You can show it to your dermatologist
If she is treating a rash, or cyst,
But hear me now: no daughter of mine
Belongs in thongs. That's the bottom line.

ⒶSSISTED ⅬIVING

I'm sick of this house and making repairs,
Mowing the lawn, climbing the stairs,
So when the A.C. went on the fritz
The same week the refrigerator quits
And the roof springs a leak
And cockroaches come, all in one week,
I took my wife, Lulubelle,
And we moved to the St. Paul Hotel.
Three thousand a week and they treat us quite well.
Cashed in the house and the 401(k)
And the money should last until Labor Day.
They gave us the honeymoon suite,
A king-size bed with French linen sheets.
"Any special requests?" they said. "Yes, champagne.
A Caesar salad and quiche Lorraine
And maybe a bottle of your best Merlot."
We're living high, spare no expense.
Any problems, call Maintenance.
A privileged life fit for a prince.
Every day fresh towels, fresh sheets, two mints.
No need for a car, there's a cab at the curb.
Nobody bothers us: *Do Not Disturb.*

When we get all we can get

And the money runs out and we're in debt

And they throw us out the door, no sweat.

We're still on Easy Street: what gives?

We'll go and live with our relatives,

Who are Christians just like us,

All brought up to be generous

Especially to the poor,

And that will be us, for sure.

Jesus said, "What you do for the poor you do for me."

In other words, we're divinity.

Last Words

On a chill November day
Boughs are bare, the sky is gray,
Windows are dark, people look sad,
The talk is slow, the food is bad.
I walk across the dying lawn
And think of those who have passed on.
Those who reached the riverside
And launched out upon the tide,
Passing to yon distant shore,
Wishing for a few years more.

As they lay on their deathbed,
A cold compress on their forehead,
Their relatives standing by,
Smiling, trying not to cry,
And a nurse stood there, discreet,
Waiting to pull up the sheet,
And a priest kept solemn watch
While wishing for a glass of Scotch,
The dying person, feverish, thought
About their life now almost done
And why didn't they have more fun?
"Why didn't I cut loose and live?
Why was I so conservative
And worried about my expenses,
Verb tenses, self-defenses,
The economic consequences,

Always taking the lowest bids?

Why did I leave so much to my kids?

Why didn't I ride the carousel,

Spend the winter in Cozumel,

Stay at the Ritz and not the Super 6 Motel?

Why did I treat those brats so well?

God damn it to hell."

And then comes the death knell,

And it's a fire alarm bell

And a bitter sulfur smell

And the shrieks of an infidel,

And he thinks, "Our Father Who art"

But his lips don't part,

He's lost his heart.

There is no beat.

Up comes the sheet.

Long, Long Ago

Do you remember way back in '22,
Back when the sun used to shine.
Then climate changed and the volcanoes blew
And now it's dark as a mine.
Icebergs melted and up rose the sea,
Florida became a reef.
Tips of antennas where New York used to be,
But Washington's gone: a relief.

They put antidepressants now in latte
And gender's no longer clear-cut.
There's M and F but most folks are They
Except for a few who are What.
No one reads books, you just buy an app
And attach it to your forehead
And in less than a minute, you hear a snap
And all of Proust has been read.
Not like it was long ago.
I'm old. I know.

Remember the iPods that we used to use
Back in 2006.
Listened to music, downloaded the news,
And we subscribed to Netflix.
Now they just alter your genetic chain,
Millions of gigabytes flow to your brain,
Music and news and a drug for the pain,
Not like it was long ago.
Sometimes I long for how it used to be
When you and I sat on the grass by a tree

And we two conversed quietly
With a sense of mystery.
Now we are online twenty-four hours,
Wired to higher digital powers,
Receiving signals from satellite towers,
Cameras concealed in sunflowers.

Got drugs to be happy, drugs to lose weight,
Some bring you up and others sedate.
I am nostalgic for 2008
Back in the long, long ago.
So I took a boat to an island off Maine
Where the Wi-Fi antenna collapsed in the rain.
Maybe I'm dreaming or else I'm insane,
But it's lovely and I can't complain.
Nothing to do but think of you, kid.
AI is doing the work I once did.
"Write a poem about missing the past,"
I said and it came in one minute. Fast.
It's writing my memoir, I'm having a blast.
But I miss you, I must confess,
So put my name in your GPS
And an Uber launch will dock.
We'll sit on a porch and actually talk
Back and forth, no texting. We'll laugh.
I have a fine old phonograph,
And we'll listen to rock 'n' roll and we'll play
Scrabble as we did back in the day.
Message 48286x4A
Sent 6/5 by AIV system
Read @ 8:40 pm

Way Out West

On a summer day in a cool car
Driving with the top down on Sunset Boulevard,
Past the old Columbia studio,
Home of Curly, Larry, and Moe,
The iron gate they walked through:
Nyuk nyuk nyuk. Woo woo woo.
Past the Roosevelt Hotel and at Sunset & Vine
You look up and see the Hollywood sign.
In-N-Out Burger, Tarot reading, a strip club *Girls Girls Girls*,
On a neon sign that flashes as it twirls.
And beyond the neon signs and the gin mills
The sculpted hedges of Beverly Hills
And houses like reinforced stockades
In Bel Air and Pacific Palisades.
Then the Pacific Coast Highway and you end your run
At the beach looking at the setting sun.
And what more is there to say?
You've come to the end of the U.S.A.
No dictation or
devotion to promotion,
Locomotion, information, or notion of nation,
Just crustaceans and the motions of ocean

GRADUATION

The kids graduated and now they are gone,
Lindsay and Megan and Kevin and Sean,
Four graduations and plenty of tears
And now we are launched on our post-parent years.

This lady and I were once paramours;
She spent thirty years cleaning toilets and floors.
I remember her skin so pale and so soft;
I intend to take up right where we left off.

We'll be lovers once more and not cops and chauffeurs.
We'll enjoy all the foods to which kids were averse,
Oysters, artichokes, steak rare and red,
As we tune in the Stones and the Grateful Dead.

We've thrown all our parenting books away.
We're done forever with the P.T.A.
Years of soccer reach a merciful end
And we'll never ever go camping again.

Good luck to you, Sean, on Graduation Day.
Hope to see you for Christmas, but if not, okay.
Here's a check for two grand, don't spend it all at once.
Now we're off to Paris for a couple of months.

We've sold the house; enough is enough.
You have until August to clean out your stuff.
We've looked at our options and gotten a lease
On a very nice two-bedroom flat in Nice.

We're studying French and I must say, "*C'est bon!*"
We're going to be hermits, no TV, no phone,
No forwarding address, no Wi-Fi, no car.
"*C'est la vie, ma famille,*" we say. "*Au revoir.*"

THE AFTERLIFE

Mother, Mother, tell the truth,
What happens when I lose my youth?
"Child, child, who can tell?
You might die, you might do well."
Mother called the doctor,
Doctor called the nurse,
The nurse she called the priest
From the Catholic church.
"Fatal," said the doctor.
"Fatal," said the nurse.
"Tell me," said the priest.
"When were you last in church?"
I was there last Sunday
And I confessed my sins.
"Did you confess the time
You made love with Corinne?"
Yes, I did confess it. Why?
"Did you cross your heart and hope to die?"
That I have no memory of.
"How many times did you make love?"
1 2 3 4 5 6 7.
Tell me, will I go to heaven?
"Do you believe in the Father, Son,
Holy Ghost, the three in one?"
Yes, my Father, yes I do.
"And which church did you go to?"
I went to the church of open air,
The apple tree and peach and pear,

The grass and flowers and leafy mist.

"Then go and ask a botanist."

The botanist said, "When you die

And deep down in the ground you lie,

When you're shriveled up and shrunk,

And your stink is completely stunk,

Then from in your lower spine

There will rise a slender trunk

And you'll become a lonesome pine.

I believe that every sinner'll

Come back vegetable, not mineral,

But before that comes to pass,

You must become a cloud of gas.

But in the end you'll always be

Another branch of the family."

My Old Man

Daddy was a gardener,
He loved his corn and peas,
The strawberry beds he kept
While tending all the apple trees.
Tomatoes, melons, row by row
He cultivated with his hoe.
I think of him in the sun,
Mowing the yard till it was done.

Daddy was a carpenter,
He loved to cut and trim.
Whenever I hear a power saw
I always think of him,
Nails in his mouth, hammer in hand
Way up high on a ladder he'd stand.
I think of him in his coveralls
Packing up the tools as evening falls.

Once a month I sat on a chair
With his big hand on my head
And he carefully cut my hair
As clean and true as a carpenter could do.

Daddy liked to work on cars,
Open up the hood,
Adjust the timing, tighten the belt,
Grease the bearings good.
He and my uncles looked at cars
Parked in the driveway
And never tired of arguing
About Ford vs. Chevrolet.

He died in the house he built
And we carried him through town
In a long black Cadillac
And we laid him in the ground.
I think of him when I happen to say
Something he would've said
And then I feel his hand
Resting on my head.

We had few conversations,
I can't recall a one.
He was a Midwestern man
And I am his son.

I think of him when I drive a car
And when a train goes by
And when I hear the hymns he loved
Or smell a homemade pie.

The living leave, they move away,
My friends have drifted far apart
But the dead are with us every day.
On our mind and in our heart.

Ballad of an Old Man

'Twas Christmas Day in the Poorhouse
Where poor old me and you
Ate donated turkey and cranberries
Sent by the well-to-do.
And each of us paupers was given
A gift, at public expense:
Perfume for the ladies,
A bar of soap for the gents.

I looked up from my boiled spuds
And said to the warden, "Sir,
Whatever became of my daughter?
I'm expecting a visit from her."

"She's down in the Caribbean,"
The warden said with a sneer.
"Your children are rich and successful,
Why should they visit you here?
They've dinners to go to and parties,
Benefits and premieres.
Finish your dinner and go to your cell
Or I'll kick you down the stairs.

"You're old and sick and depressing
And your conversation's a bore.
You're frankly not all that attractive,
A common fate of the poor."

I went to my cell in the darkness
Where my empty stocking hung
And decided to pass on a word of advice
To you, the attractive and young.

Don't marry and do not have children,
Take buses wherever you go.
Live with your parents and revise their wills
To inherit all of their dough.
Invest in blue-chips and municipals,
Keep all the money you earn
Simply by having no address
And not filing a tax return.

Don't answer the knock on the door
Lest it be the IRS man.
When they pass the collection plate,
Take money out if you can.
Get food at the food shelf,
Steal stuff from loading docks.
You can furnish your place with stuff
You find sitting on sidewalks.
Buy your clothes at Goodwill,
Drink the $3 rosé,
Collect all the pats of butter
They bring you at the café.
And when you are old and senile
And you think that your niece is your aunt,
My dears, you'll have plenty of money,
Though you forget what you want.
As you sit in assisted living,
Read the statements from the bank,
And you'll be rolling in money
And you'll have me to thank.

THE LITERARY LIFE

I'm here to tell you people
That nothing is brighter
And slicker and nicer
Than the life of a writer.
It's true, I'm in fiction
And it is a snap.
Got dough in my pocket
And babes on my lap.
Some say writing's torture,
I'm not one of those guys.
I write in ink
And I never revise.

I never had writer's block
For more than a minute,
And every book I wrote
Had something good in it.
I take naps on the couch
With a mirror on the ceiling
So I can look up
And see how good I'm feeling.
Some writers suffer,
I have to laugh.
I write a novel
In a week and a half.

I hang out with models
And movie stars
At four-star restaurants
And exclusive bars.
I order prime rib
And some Dom Pérignon
And women lean down
And ask, "Are you alone?"
It's a wonderful life,
The life of fiction,
And love is my only addiction.
The love of my life,
Of friends good and true,
And dozens of readers like you.